Creating a Climate for Giving

Donald W. Joiner

DISCIPLESHIP RESOURCES

P.O. BOX 340003 • NASHVILLE, TN 37203-0003
www.discipleshipresources.org

Cover design by Nanci Lamar
Book design by Joey McNair
Edited by Linda R. Whited and Heidi L. Hewitt

ISBN 0-88177-318-2

Library of Congress Catalog Card No. 00-105445

DR318

Contents

It Is More Than Money

Changing the Way Your Church Funds Ministry

"**W**hat do you do?" is the question my seatmates on airplanes ask me most often. When I fly—and I fly frequently—I like my private time to meditate, think, read, and relax. Sometimes, though, I sit next to a talker. They are often afraid to fly because they think the plane may go down. Since it may be their last chance to tell their life story, talkers must discuss everything.

Sometimes I tell people I am a certified financial planner. Then they usually ask, "What is the best investment?" or "How can I get some money to invest when I usually don't have enough at the end of the month just to pay bills?" When it comes to their lives, people want to talk about money.

At other times, I tell people that I am a director of stewardship for The United Methodist Church. That usually closes the discussion. People will talk about their personal management of money, but they become strangely silent about money and the church.

Personally, I like to talk about money. I like to talk about money in the church. I have often been called a financial evangelist. That is quite a compliment where I come from. I become evangelistic (enthusiastic) about money and the church because I know what happens to the money that goes through the church, and I know what happens to people when they become givers.

Few people are natural givers or sharers. Just take a look at two toddlers playing with a pile of toys. If one child picks up a toy the other child had been playing with but has now discarded, the first child immediately wants the toy back. Giving (sharing) is a learned trait that our parents teach us.

As Christians, we learn about giving from God. The words "For God so loved the world that he gave his only Son" (John 3:16) are familiar ones that we memorized in Sunday school. For Christians, giving is not a matter of paying the bills of the church; rather, it is a response to the grace of God in Jesus Christ that has given us abundant life. When we become receivers, when we receive the gift of God in our lives, giving (sharing) becomes a natural part of who we are. Our giving, both through the church and outside the church, is a natural function of our Christian life. As the apostle Paul says, we give enthusiastically (2 Corinthians 9:7) because we can do no other.

We give through the church because we know what great things happen to those who can be receivers of God's good news. We want the world to know about Jesus Christ, our friends and neighbors to experience the grace of God in their lives, and our children to know about the love of God. We rejoice in the service of worship through the church.

As a stewardship leader for the United Methodist denomination, I see the good things that happen because of our giving through the church. When disasters such as hurricanes occur, trucks of supplies and relief aid are shipped from churches, even before the storm is finished with its devastation, to make the wrath of the storm less enduring. I see members of many churches coming together to provide support for new churches in areas where the people could not do it on their own. I see inner-city churches, such as Nashville's Hobson or Detroit's Cass Community, in vital ministries supported by a wide range of churches outside their communities. If it were up to a single church alone to fund them, those ministries would cease to exist.

Living in this society takes money, but giving through the church is about more than money. It is about lives being changed. It is about never feeling lonely or unloved. It is about helping others. It is about children and youth. It is about our personal salvation. It is about what God has done for us in Jesus Christ. It is about God's grace in our everyday lives. Giving through the church is about supporting the ministries of our church in exciting and glorious ways.

Few people are born givers. For some, being a generous giver is a gift from God; for others, it was learned from parents who modeled tithing. For most, though, giving grows because of what church leaders do, and do not do, to help people learn what it means to give.

This book is about church leaders taking responsibility not only for managing the finances of the church but also for creating Christian philanthropists. That means taking responsibility for creating systems, raising funds, and funding ministry so that church members learn to be givers and have opportunities to give with excitement for the ministry of Jesus Christ through the church.

Chapter One

Creating a Climate for Giving

Per-member giving as a percentage of after-tax income declined between 1968 and the 1990's.

(*Behind the Stained Glass Windows: Money Dynamics in the Church,* by John and Sylvia Ronsvalle; Baker Books, 1996; page 17. Used by permission.)

Giving patterns in the United States indicate the church is losing market share among its own members.

(*Behind the Stained Glass Windows: Money Dynamics in the Church,* by John and Sylvia Ronsvalle; Baker Books, 1996; page 29. Used by permission.)

According to an article in the *New York Times,* an annual study by Newtithing Group, a San Francisco-based philanthropic research organization, estimates that...U.S. tax filers can comfortably afford to donate nearly a quarter of a trillion [$242 billion] additional dollars to charity.

(*Fund Raising Management Magazine,* May 1999, page 3. © *Fund Raising Management Magazine.* Used by permission.)

In the year 2000, more than $200 billion will be given to all charities in the United States alone.

(Donald W. Joiner, General Board of Discipleship. Used by permission.)

By the year 2020, more than $30 trillion will be passed from one generation to another through estate transfers.

(Donald W. Joiner, General Board of Discipleship. Used by permission.)

A recent study found that the number-one issue for the local church is stewardship. What is really meant is financial stewardship. The church is experiencing tight money. The same cry is heard in the local church, at the conference level, and across the nation: "Help! The same old ways are no longer working!"

"The times, they are a-changing" is not just a slogan from the 1960's but is a real part of financial stewardship today. Maybe there was a time (in ancient church history) when people had no other place to give (time or finances) than through the church. During those times the church had only to say, "We need...," and enough money came in. A few remnants of that remain in churches today, but fewer and fewer people are responding to that type of fundraising.

Today, charitable giving is big business. In 2000, charitable donations for all causes in the United States will exceed $200 billion. With federal, state, and local governments progressively getting out of community work, more organizations have come into being to meet needs. Churches may fool themselves into thinking they do not have competition for donated dollars, but the truth is that the person in the pew, not the non-church person, gives to charitable causes. Data also shows that more and more people are giving to more than one local congregation, sometimes in the same community. Not only is your local church in competition with other charities, but the church is also up against the competitive, consumptive society in which we live—with local sporting events, school activities, fast-food restaurants, and cable television.

Many church leaders think about financial stewardship the same way they have for the past fifty years. Financial stewardship is not a new issue; it has just caught up with us. My observations suggest that symptoms of tight money began showing up in the early 1980's. The church solved the problem by cutting programs and pinching pennies. Today, our problem is that we have cut as much as we can, and we have pinched as much as we can. Where do we go from here?

One central idea that emerges from the Total Quality Management movement is the idea that a system delivers the results it is designed for (*Quest for Quality in the Church: A New Paradigm,* by Ezra Earl Jones; Discipleship Resources, 1993; page 21). Are you satisfied with the results your church is getting in giving? in attendance? in participation? in membership? Every organization, including the church, has one or more systems out of which it operates. Systems can be either positive or negative.

> ## Systems
>
> A system is a perceived whole whose elements "hang together" because they continually affect each other over time and operate toward a common purpose.... Examples of systems include biological organisms (including human bodies), the atmosphere, diseases, ecological niches, factories, chemical reactions, political entities, communities, industries, families, teams—and all organizations.
>
> (*The Fifth Discipline Fieldbook: Strategies and Tools for Building a Learning Organization,* by Peter M. Senge, Charlotte Roberts, Richard B. Ross, Bryan J. Smith, Art Kleiner; Doubleday, 1994; page 90. Used by permission.)

Systems create a climate for people to respond favorably or unfavorably to the church. Each local congregation has a financial system that encourages or discourages giving, receives gifts, and manages gifts. It is easy to design and promote an excellent annual commitment campaign that is guaranteed to increase commitments. However, if the church's system does not create a climate for giving, no program will solve the problem of tight money.

Most church financial systems focus on money—and getting it into the church. The goal seems to be to find ways to get members to give, even when leaders perceive that people do not want to give. When this negative philosophy guides church finance, the focus is on money and the needs of the church. Being sure that everyone sees the budget or financial statistics is paramount. Sometimes, money that is given for special causes is spent on bills instead of mission. That is fraud!

Finance committees and local church leaders must see the solution to the financial needs as a systems concern, not a program concern. In the past, we identified the problem (not enough money because members are not giving) and designed a program to solve the problem (an annual fund campaign). The guiding theology—if you can call it that— that directs this kind of system is that people do not want to give. After all, "They have worked hard for all they have, and they have a right to spend it as they please. They do not want to spend it at the church." Therefore, we design gimmicks and ploys to get people to give up their money. The image is one of a tight fist, with the church trying to pry the fingers open to get to the money. The finance committee may describe the process of raising the budget as getting blood out of a turnip.

In some churches, vocal members who do not yet enjoy the excitement of being faithful givers are chosen as finance leaders. Many have never been faced with giving from a viewpoint of faith instead of from a checkbook balance. They have convinced other leaders that people are not able to give more. Therefore, they avoid giving issues, shy away from talking about tithing, and design low-key finance campaigns. By the systems churches design and the processes they follow, they are raising members for whom giving is a bad word and an issue to avoid.

With a fundraising philosophy, a church will focus on stewardship strictly as money. The only time people will hear the word *stewardship* is when church leaders are short on funds and are looking for ways to pay bills. Stewardship includes giving money; but when that is all it is, it is nothing more than a religious gimmick to get more money out of people in order to pay bills. Stewardship is then forgotten until church leaders again need money, or until the fall campaign. In time, members feel used. Giving is taken out of the realm of a faith response and becomes a token response.

Fundraising philosophies also focus on the limited amount of resources a congregation has. Few financial leaders encompass visions further than a ledger book. Most see only a limited amount of money available to pay bills. Those who try to lead the church by vision, rather than by disaster, are faced with systems that do not allow them to be faithful leaders, let alone faithful givers. Church leaders talk about we-and-them problems. Their discussions focus on how "we" can get "them" to give, or on how "we" can assess the inactives a minimum measure of support.

A Tale of Two Churches

The following is a composite picture of two churches from my own recent studies. (Note: Because of space limitations, we will describe only the financial pictures of these two churches.)

The first church, First Old Paradigm Church, is struggling to pay bills. In spite of the rapid changes in the church during the past twenty years, they are still living and responding as they have for fifty years.

The second church, Hope New Paradigm Church, has a vibrant ministry, a packed sanctuary for worship, and fully funded ministries. In fact, last year Hope New Paradigm Church gave 43 percent of their budget to missions and had a cash reserve at the end of the year of $43,000.

First Old Paradigm Church

First Old Paradigm is the same church it was twenty years ago. In fact, the same leaders hold positions they held when things were going well for the church. The following are some characteristics of First Old Paradigm's fundraising program:

- They send everyone a copy of the budget.
- They place statistics of giving in the bulletin each week.
- They have no finance campaign, or a low-key approach.
- They have a giving attitude that says it is between the giver and God.
- They keep all giving records secret.
- They tell the congregation about finances only at certain times:
  a. in December in order to pay end-of-year bills,
  b. at the time of a finance campaign,
  c. at the time of financial emergencies.
- They claim that their vision for ministry is the same as other churches'.
- They designate little money for missions.
- They discourage gifts to endowments (detracts from the general fund).
- They discourage designated giving (finance committee should decide).
- They put all gifts from estates and memorials into the general budget.
- They have clergy who separate themselves from financial work and do not want to know what people give.
- They report that they are keeping the budget the same as last year's.
- They use primary vocabulary: *loyalty* and *obligation.*
- They send statements and envelopes only to those who pledge.
- They think that giving should be to the church and not to the outside.
- They suggest that everyone should live a simple life and give extra to the church.
- They are proud that members give when they are asked to give.

Hope New Paradigm Church

Hope New Paradigm Church was founded more than 133 years ago. In the past five years, their membership has increased 33 percent, and their worship attendance has increased 48 percent. The following are some characteristics of Hope New Paradigm Church's fund-development ministry:

- They know why they are in ministry and have a vision to guide them.
- They have a budget to guide them, not to dictate ministry or program.
- They recognize the offering as a time to celebrate God's ministry.

- They have no annual finance campaign as such, but they
  a. invite people to tithe,
  b. encourage giving to special causes,
  c. invite commitment and growth in giving as part of spiritual development.
- They have people witness every Sunday about their giving or about what the church's ministry has done for them.
- They send envelopes to all people monthly (including a development brochure about where funds are allowing ministry to happen that month).
- They encourage all people to consider their assets as part of their stewardship and giving.
- They view giving as sacramental rather than as sacrificial.
- They celebrate memorial and honor gifts.
- They encourage endowment and capital giving from assets.
- They have an active program of Christian financial planning.
- They have a pastor who preaches about stewardship regularly and with excitement.
- They give 43 percent of the budget to missions, with a goal to increase that by 2 percent annually until they are giving more to missions than to themselves.
- They have both a pastor and a finance committee who know and keep track of giving/attendance/participation records as vital signs of congregational and individual spiritual health.
- They give as an act of faith, rather than as a way to finance the budget.

Recognizing Myths

Myths are supposed truths that lead church leaders to go in the wrong direction. Consider the experiences of First Old Paradigm Church and Hope New Paradigm Church as you think about some of the many myths that influence church finance leaders. These myths, when they become the operational guidelines (or system) by which financial decisions are made in the church, lead churches to a negative fundraising philosophy.

When we expose these myths as untrue, a new finance system can be designed that moves the church from fundraising to fund development, from paying bills to giving birth to Christian philanthropists.

What are some of the most common financial myths found in churches today? To focus on the process, we will look at some myths that lead to a fundraising philosophy.

Fundraising Myths
- Ownership in the Individual
- Focus on Institution
- Focus on Money
- Focus on Budget
- Focus on Member/Obligation
- Focus on Shortfall

Ownership in the Individual

The first myth is that the money people have is theirs, and that they can do whatever they want with it. Although the church affirms that what we have is God's, we act as though we really do not believe it. We accept our society's theology—if you can call it that—that affirms each individual person's ownership of what he or she has.

Focus on Institution

Another myth is that the most important thing is to show that the church (the institution) needs people's money. Another is that God needs their giving. Does God need people's money, or do people need to give as a response to what God has done?

Focus on Money

It is a natural conclusion for finance leaders to believe the myth that the most important thing is money. The more church leaders become involved in financial statements and budget development, the more they fall into the trap of seeing only money issues instead of the overall vision of the church.

Focus on Budget

A similar myth is that all we need to do is tell people how the money is being spent. If we report how much it costs, where the money is going (that is, the budget), and how much more we need, then people will give accordingly. We believe that if we just show the numbers (reports in bulletins or newsletters), people will respond. The truth is that information without invitation (to respond) moves few people to action.

Focus on Member/Obligation

A prominent myth among financially unhealthy churches is that all we need to do is remind people about the commitment they made to support the church with their service, time, talents, and gifts when they joined the church. A myth that goes along with this is that if we make people feel guilty, they will give.

Focus on Shortfall

One myth that seems to get some response from members is that the money just comes in when we tell them we need it. The system that is developed out of this myth gives birth not to givers but to responders who will pay when you ask, and nothing more. In this kind of congregation, members feel that the church is always asking for money. Members give out of loyalty or obligation. They are blamed for not giving enough, and financial crises are frequent. I call this the TV Evangelist Fundraising System: "If you don't give so much by a certain date, the church will close." Who wants to give, or give generously, to a church that may close?

These myths give rise to assumptions that govern the financial system of many local congregations. These assumptions are accepted as fact, are not tested, are handed down from one generation of leaders to the next, and are part of the system that discourages giving.

Some Assumptions That Have Negative Results

1. If people feel sufficiently guilty, they will give.
2. People are basically stingy and extremely protective of their money.
3. If you tell people the church needs money, they will give.
4. Asking for financial commitment will drive people away.
5. When people join the church, they are fully committed to giving to the church.
6. What people put on their commitment card is the most they will give to the church.
7. The church's income is tied to the income of its members.

A speaker at a national stewardship conference a couple years ago said that most giving to the church is not charitable. That made me feel a little defensive and ready to argue. I wanted to mention the parable of the widow's mite (equal sacrifice, not equal giving); but when I thought about what he was saying, I began to agree with him. When we spend a minimum of $5.00 at a fast-food restaurant, at least $1.25 for a soft drink or coffee; and $7.50 per person at a movie theater (and another $5.00 per person at the concession stand)—and when we think that cable television, power windows and door locks, and air conditioning are necessities—giving a dollar to the church is not charitable giving. This is not all the fault of the members.

A New Paradigm

A new paradigm (way of operation) influenced by a balanced understanding of stewardship focuses not on the church but on the individual. People need to give. Christian stewards want to give. How can church leaders help stewards respond to the call of God in their lives?

The new paradigm turns away from fundraising and focuses on funding ministry. Notice how the new paradigm of funding ministry is different from the myths that lead to fundraising.

Fundraising	Funding Ministry
• Ownership in the Individual	• God's Ownership
• Focus on Institution	• Focus on the Individual
• Focus on Money	• Focus on Ministry
• Focus on Budget	• Focus on Results
• Focus on Member/Obligation	• Focus on Donor Relationship
• Focus on Shortfall	• Focus on Possibilities

God's Ownership

Stewardship with a funding-ministry philosophy will focus not on our ownership but on God's ownership.

Focus on the Individual

Stewardship with a funding-ministry philosophy will focus not on the institution but on the individual. Relationships and spiritual growth are more important than how much a member can do for the church. People rather than programs are at the center of the church's ministry.

Focus on Ministry

Stewardship with a funding-ministry philosophy will focus not on money and the need of the church to receive it but on ministry. The church celebrates faith development over membership growth.

Focus on Results

Stewardship with a funding-ministry philosophy will focus not on the budget and how much we need to raise but on the results of ministry.

Focus on Donor Relationship

Stewardship with a funding-ministry philosophy will focus not on membership obligation and loyalty but on donor relationship. Instead of members living up to the vows they took when they joined the church (prayers, presence, gifts, and service), the focus is on the faithful response of the members. The members have a choice in where they give and how much. The goal is birthing Christian philanthropists more than fulfilling membership vows.

Focus on Possibilities

Stewardship with a funding-ministry philosophy will focus not on shortfall, crises, and survival but on possibilities, the future, and reaching out.

Funding-ministry thinking gives rise to some new stewardship principles that may replace the assumptions of fundraising thinking.

Stewardship Principles for Funding Ministry

1. People who are part of our churches are there because of a response to a spiritual quest in their lives to find meaning in God.
2. Christian stewards have not reached the apex of their spiritual journey.
3. Christian stewards who have received the love of God in their lives want and need to give.
4. The need of a person to give, or share, is more basic than the need of the church to receive.
5. Understanding oneself as a steward requires no less than a conversion of attitude toward one's possessions.
6. People enjoy knowing what monetary transactions make possible.
7. The church that knows what God wants them to do (vision) will have an easier time funding the ministry for which that church is called.
8. The church that thinks of money positively will find ways to help people give.
9. A church whose leaders are on a spiritual journey (exemplified in their giving, attendance, participation, prayer life) are part of a financially healthy congregation. In other words, when the leaders lead, the congregation will follow (Joiner's Law).
10. A church's stewardship will influence the members' stewardship.
11. A pastor who models giving will find a congregation following that lead.

> What assumptions guide the funding system of
> your church?
> -
> -
> -
> -
> -
> -

The old paradigm identified external problems as the cause of decreased giving:
- people (inadequate commitment);
- economy (not enough money);
- age (all our people are on fixed incomes);
- politics (do not like what the general church is doing).

The cause of decreased giving is not people. It is not the economy. It is not even lack of money. The reason people are not giving is that the system has created a climate for people to give elsewhere. I think people want to give. If you believe that, the giving climate in your church will change. If you shift the focus away from the church and toward helping people fulfill their giving needs, the church will prosper. Any congregation has enough money to do everything God wants the church to do. That is the new paradigm.

Instead of sitting in meetings complaining about members' lack of commitment, instead of seeking ways to get non-givers to give, instead of centering on what's wrong, focus on what has been done to discourage giving. That is the new paradigm.

Focus on the givers or the beneficiaries of your church's ministries, not on budgets or money. What are the results of giving? How are people's lives touched by the ministries of your church? That is the new paradigm.

Instead of giving a stewardship report on the money that is needed to pay bills, give someone a chance to tell why he or she is a member of the church. In one church, an eight-year-old girl named Esther stood before the congregation and thanked them for the Bibles given to her third grade class. She said, "That is the only Bible in our home." That is the new paradigm.

When people see the results of ministry, their giving takes on a new climate of excitement and celebration. When giving theology shifts from people hoarding their money to celebrating a covenant or partnership with God, people become excited about giving. That is the new paradigm.

Chapter Two

Developing a Strategy for Funding Ministry

The solution to the financial problems of local churches can be summarized in three common statements I hear from finance leaders:

1. If people were just more committed...
2. If we give people the right information...
3. If we just had the right program...

Nothing is solved in three easy steps, let alone one of the above steps. Each of the statements has a degree of truth, but no one solution by itself will solve any church's financial problems.

The most common statement I hear from finance leaders is, "If our people were just more committed..." When I hear that kind of statement, I groan. The questions to ask are, "Committed to what?" and "How do we judge a person's commitment?" A person's commitment to God, as God is known in Jesus Christ, and commitment to the values, mission, and vision of the church are certainly important to any giving environment. If we neglect the spiritual growth of individuals, we may find their giving lacking in many ways. The financial leaders of the church often assume that this vital part of the church's life is handled by others. However, the work churches do in funding ministry cannot be seen apart from the total life of the congregation. An intentional ministry of developing Christian philanthropists and stewards is integral to the ongoing ministry of all churches.

What is a philanthropist? A philanthropist is often thought of as a person who has given a large amount of money, with the emphasis on the amount of money given instead of on the charity to which it is given. Philanthropy is not about how much one gives but about the nature of how one feels or the motivation one has for giving. The dictionary defines a philanthropist as one who has a desire to help humanity. To develop Christian philanthropists, we focus on their role as stewards. When we assist them in moving from an idea of their ownership to God's ownership, when they move from singleness in life ("I can do it myself") to a partnership with God, life takes on new meaning. Earning, gathering, and giving take on an exciting atmosphere.

Commitment by itself is never enough. We have people in our churches whose commitment cannot be challenged, yet they are among the people who give the least to the church—both in actual dollars and in relation to the resources available to them. Commitment without focus and direction does not necessarily produce givers, at least not people who give to your church. I believe Christians who discover their role as a steward cannot help but give. But where do they give? And why do they give?

Some finance leaders would say that all we need to do is give people the right information. That usually results in putting the budget in the hands of every member and placing the correct financial statistics of the moment in the church bulletin or newsletter. For example:

	Our Church's Numbers
$123,456	Needed to date
$96,459	Received to date
123	Worship attendance

What do these numbers mean? How will these numbers make people do anything different in their giving, or even in their attendance? People who know more about what is going on in the church's life usually give more. What kind of information moves people to respond?

Several years ago, I agreed to assume the responsibilities of the stewardship committee in the church where I worship. One of the responsibilities was to lead the fall finance campaign. We were talking about the budget, which was about $400,000, when Herb, a long-time member of the church who had retired from his job more than twenty-one years before, told us that a budget did nothing for him. He had never earned more than $18,000 in any year when he worked. There were items in the budget, he reminded us, that were more than he had been paid for a year's work. The bottom line only confused him.

At Calvary Church, the finance committee was meeting with me to discuss their financial situation. Tom, who had not been there for any of the other meetings, declared, "Just give everyone a copy of the budget, and they will know how much to give." Phil, who was chairing the meeting, responded, "That's true, Tom. After all, we on the finance committee and the church leaders have seen many copies of the budget, and all of us are tithing—right?" The committee members' eyes turned toward the table, for they knew how much they gave. Some of them came close to a tithe, but many of them were nearer the bottom of that equation. And they were the ones who knew, more than anyone else in the church, the total financial picture.

> Information without invitation produces informed members, but not necessarily givers.

I recently attended morning worship at a small rural church. Taped to the front of the pulpit was a sign announcing that the church needed just one more teacher to fulfill the church's teaching needs for the fall. The next day I asked the pastor how many people had responded to the sign. You are right. People saw the sign—just as they see the budget and the financial information in the bulletin—as information but not necessarily as an invitation to do anything.

Christian commitment may produce givers, but it may not produce gifts to the church. Information without invitation produces informed members, but it may not produce any action. Information without commitment produces bill payers. Commitment, along with the information about the church's vision and mission and its success in responding to God's call, will produce people who may consider your church in their giving plan before they give elsewhere.

Another part of producing a giving church is to provide an invitation. This is usually in the form of a finance campaign. A number of changes in this area have occurred in the past five to ten years, but most churches are still hanging onto what they have done for the past fifty years, with decreasing results.

In a recent study, I discovered that there are three kinds of churches:

1. Churches who pride themselves on not having any kind of finance campaign (and almost never talking about money and their church)— Their giving, even if all bills have been paid, is about one-third of the national average. I question what good these churches are doing for their members, or whether they are even fulfilling God's call in their own community.

2. Churches who talk about money only at the time of the finance campaign or when they need money—These churches almost never have enough to pay bills. They are barely surviving.

3. Churches who know that the focus of giving is not on the money but on the raising of Christian stewards who are blessed givers, not to the church but through the church, for God's work—These churches always talk about financial stewardship in terms that focus on a faithful response to God's actions. They do not shy away from discussing issues of faithful giving or about inviting members to be part of God's plan through that church.

A finance campaign or an annual commitment program by itself will rarely solve any church's financial problems. However, members will give elsewhere if the church does not give them an opportunity to respond to what they are feeling in their hearts, and if it does not have a plan to allow them to commit to that heart-felt call in their lives.

Money is not the issue!

If churches are to reach the members of this new millennium and finance the ministries God is calling us to accomplish in making disciples, it is time to evaluate what we are doing, make prescriptions for change, and develop a new strategy for funding ministry. To fail to develop this comprehensive plan is to guarantee that churches will not survive the coming age.

It is time to throw out the old ways that no longer are working and to develop a comprehensive, long-range, faith-based strategy. This new strategy must take into account developing committed Christians who are informed about the ministries of their church and who are excited about being generous, faithful Christian philanthropists. Such a comprehensive strategy will focus on the following:
1. Developing a faith community that understands and gratefully grasps the concept of being Christian stewards;
2. Sharing ministry with excited Christian philanthropists;
3. Providing opportunities to respond in giving;
4. Having a ministry that is more interested in caring for members than in how much money the members give;
5. Realizing that giving goes beyond the morning offering.

Several churches I studied recently were in the process of using Wayne Barrett's book *Get Well! Stay Well! Prescriptions for a Financially Healthy Congregation* (Nashville: Discipleship Resources, 1997) as a guide to developing a comprehensive strategy for funding ministry. Trinity Church used the book to study their church's stewardship program. Mary called it a stewardship audit of their church. They were embarrassed at the results, so they designed a comprehensive, year-round plan to increase the level of stewardship in their congregation. The goals listed on page 26 became the focus of their comprehensive plan.

Comprehensive Stewardship Plan

Goal: Commitment
a. Teach faith-based giving, starting with church leaders.
b. Have an emphasis on tithing once a year.
c. Assist people to know what gifts for ministry they have and to find ways to implement those gifts.
d. Focus on the need of the giver to give (Christian philanthropy), rather than on the church's need to receive.

Goal: Information
a. Be intentional about telling stories of the work and ministry of the church.
b. Include every Sunday either an article in the bulletin on giving or a speaker.
c. Be intentional about telling the story of the church's ministry (articles in newsletters, letters to the congregation, and public relations in the community).
d. Work with the endowment committee to inform members of what and how they can give from their assets and estates.

Goal: Invitation
a. Have an annual campaign based on giving rather than on raising the budget.
b. Highlight giving beyond the budget at least four times a year.
c. Base all stewardship programs and communications on a stewardship response, not on a finance response.
d. Stop trying to design your own finance campaign. (Use a program with a proven record.)
e. Send quarterly statements of giving, along with an envelope and an invitation to give.

Each congregation is different. What worked at Trinity Church may not work in your church. Do a stewardship audit of your church to help you form your own comprehensive stewardship plan. Your first step should be to consider the theology for your funding ministry.

Chapter Three

Developing a Theology of funding Ministry

In spite of the occasional sermon or teaching about stewardship, most church people remain ill informed about the matter.

(*How to Increase Giving in Your Church*, by George Barna, page 77. © 1997 by George Barna. Used by permission of Regal Books, Ventura, CA 93003.)

Most adults who attend church services have, at best, a muddled and rudimentary understanding of money and stewardship.

(*How to Increase Giving in Your Church*, by George Barna, page 90. © 1997 by George Barna. Used by permission of Regal Books, Ventura, CA 93003.)

Most people say they believe in stewardship, but when pushed to define it, they have no clue. The church has often focused on using the term *stewardship* only during fall finance campaigns; therefore, it is not surprising that church people think of *stewardship* as a code word for getting them to give. When the newsletter or the sign in front of the church announces that it is Stewardship Sunday, people either stay away or resign themselves to hearing something about giving.

People who are part of the church have many definitions of steward-ship. When stewardship committee members are asked for their understanding of stewardship, the responses vary from trustee, to money, to custodian, to tithing. For a committee of three, there will be at least five separate understandings of stewardship. When asked what steward-ship means, a committee will often refer to the three *T's*—time, talent, treasure—a summary that limits the understanding even more.

Outside the church there are yet other definitions of stewardship. Bank officers use the term *stewardship* to refer to the fiduciary responsi-bility they have for funds that are not their own but are deposited in their bank. City officials use the term in reference to the trust placed in them by the electorate. Environmentalists see the responsibility of taking care of the environment as an act of stewardship. A youth group was asked what they thought of the words *steward* and *stewardship*. After they thought for a long time, the only thing they could think of was a wine steward (said by two), or "What about a stewardess in an air-plane?" When asked if they had heard about the word in church, they all said no.

What About You and Your Church?

> What do you think the word *stewardship* means?

> When your church plans stewardship work, what message does the approach to stewardship give to the members of the church?

KEY

Remember that the way your church defines stewardship will direct the way your church plans its ministry of stewardship.

The problem with understanding stewardship is not that the w *stewardship* is inappropriate but that we have trained people to re only a limited understanding of the term. When you define stewardship only in terms of money—even though you may say that it is more than money—then you will focus your ministry of stewardship development on money, budgets, shortfalls, crises, and the reasons that people never seem to be giving their fair share. Discussions in finance committees and in church council meetings will focus on how to get people to give more when they do not want to. The most common question church leaders in this type of church ask is, "How can we get the non-givers (that is, the inactives) to give?"

When you define stewardship in light of money, you will see the role of steward as a manager, much like a bank manager. You will begin your understanding with an inventory of what people have and how well they manage their worth. You will judge a person to be a good steward by what he or she has and by what that person gives to the church. You will build your stewardship vocabulary with words such as *loyalty, obligation,* and *sacrifice.* You will implore people to be good stewards and to live simply. You will decry the ongoing consumer culture and invite people, "if they are good Christians," to give it all to the church. When you define stewardship in this light, the only times you will approach people about their stewardship is when it is time for the fall campaign or when there is a crisis and shortfall in income for paying the bills. If the bills are paid, you will say nothing.

On the other hand, if you see stewardship in light of its spiritual focus, you will recognize stewardship as a relational concept. You will be more interested in each person than in what he or she can do for you or the church. You and your church will be more interested in the spiritual development of each person than in what he or she can do or give to the church.

The mistake in most attempts to define stewardship beyond money is to look at cultural models rather than at faith models. The most common understanding of the word *steward* is the dictionary's definition as a person who manages property, finances, or other affairs for someone else. Sometimes we refer to the early use in England of the word *stigweard,* which was the person who took care of pigs. Pigs represented wealth, so the person chosen to be a stigweard had to be highly trusted. These secular definitions of steward (or stewardship) allow humans to think that what we have is ours, even if it belongs to someone else. After all, who is that someone else?

Which of these understandings will govern the way we lead the stewards in our care? The secular definitions provide some good understandings of stewards and stewardship, but what do they say about faith and about people in the church? Are church people simply managers of something that is not their own? Or is there something more and different about being a Christian steward?

The definition of stewardship by Clarence Stoughton, said long ago, still rings true for stewardship committees and even finance campaigns:

[Stewardship is] what I do after I have said, "I believe."

(Reprinted from *A Theology for Christian Stewardship,* by T. A. Kantonen, page 90. © 1956 Muhlenberg Press. Used by permission of Augsburg Fortress.)

Unfortunately, talk about stewardship in the church has been corrupted to mean money, and our reflex action causes us to hold onto our wallets or purses as if they would suddenly disappear. Have you heard the story about two men stranded on a desert island? One seemed cheerful and upbeat; the other was nervous and dispirited. The second man spoke first, "Why are you so happy? Don't you know we'll never be found? We'll both surely die on this forsaken island." "Cheer up," replied the first man. "We'll be just fine. My church pledge is due next week, and I know the finance committee will find me!"

The word used in the Bible for *stewardship* comes from the Greek word *oikonomia.* It refers to the management of a household (Luke 12:42). For God's people, that household is more than a building with a roof, walls, windows, and a door. That household is the relationship of everyone within it. It is all people looking out for one another. Paul used *oikonomia* when he spoke of the commission God gives for the management of our whole lives (1 Corinthians 9:17). For Christians, the household is the household of faith—all of us together in a common goal. Jesus came to give us a glimpse of that goal.

Christian Stewardship Begins With God's Love

Most church definitions of stewardship begin where a secular understanding of stewardship begins, with an inventory of what we have. A Christian understanding of stewardship, however, does not begin with what we have or even how well we are managing what we have. A Christian understanding of stewardship begins with God. John 3:16, that verse we memorized in Sunday school, is the place the Christian steward begins in understanding what the word means: "God so loved the world [that's us] that he gave his only Son, so that everyone who believes in him may not perish but may have eternal life." Christian stewardship begins with God's giving. A person cannot be a Christian giver until he or she first becomes a receiver, until he or she receives God's gift.

When I was doing research several years ago for a book I was writing on Christian money management, one word that came up quite frequently in defining steward was the word *trustee.* In researching that word, I found that one explanation of its origins traces back to the Vikings (not the Minnesota football team, but the Vikings who explored the world). Before they went about their explorations, they surveyed the population. They chose the person who knew them intimately: who knew their children by name; who, if they were farmers, knew how to care for their crops; who, if they were shepherds, knew how to care for their herds. That person knew them and shared their values in life. We usually take that kind of person and put him or her in front to lead us; however, the Vikings did just the opposite. They left that person behind to take care of all that was important to them. Understanding ourselves as stewards is like that. As Christian stewards, we are God's trustees who are chosen to take care of all that is important to God.

Joseph was like that. You remember the story of Joseph, don't you? He was the seventeen-year-old boy who had the coat of many colors. His brothers, in a jealous fit, took the coat and tossed him into a pit. That is where most of us leave him. Do you remember what happened next? Joseph came out of the pit to become the second-most-important person in Egypt. Only the Pharaoh was more important. What made Joseph important? He had such an intimate relationship with God that he could interpret the Pharaoh's dreams and knew there would be years of wealth and prosperity, followed by years of famine. As a result of Joseph's relationship with God, he was chosen by Pharaoh to manage everything in the land of Egypt. Because of Joseph's stewarding, Egypt was prepared for anything. The Christian steward, like Joseph, is one who cultivates an intimate relationship with God. It is a relationship of prayer, Bible study, spiritual growth, constancy in worship, service to the community, and giving.

Yes, Christian stewardship begins with God's love, but it goes on to affirm God's ownership. When we design our ministry from a secular definition of stewardship, we accept the secular understanding that everything a person has is his or her own. A Christian understanding of stewardship, however, affirms that all we have is God's. A friend once designed an overhead slide for me to use in seminars. It shows a hearse with a rental truck on the back. How much of what we have is really ours?

Living in Tennessee, I hear constant references to the Scopes Trial (1925), which argued between evolution and Creation. I have found that each time I read the Scriptures, God speaks to me in a different way, and I id new understandings for my life. In one of my readings of the story of Creation (Genesis 1–2), I was reminded that the story of Creation is also the story of ownership. God created, we did not. One of the reasons we need to celebrate Christmas and Easter every year, and a reason we need to celebrate Holy Communion, is constantly to remind ourselves of the story of what God has done for us. Without rehearsing the story, we forget it. One of our problems is that we have failed to rehearse the story of Creation.

My mother lives in Florida. During one visit we were walking through a tourist area filled with stores. Have you noticed that we now display our philosophies of life on T-shirts and sweatshirts? One store had a T-shirt in the window with the statement "The one who dies with the most toys wins." That seems to exemplify the secular understanding of life. But how much of what we have is really ours? The Gospel of John begins with a reminder that all things came into being through God. One of the problems with tithing is that we have focused too much on the 10 percent. We believe that once we have given our 10 percent, we have done our duty. Tithing is not about giving 10 percent; it is about who we are, whose we are, and what we are doing with all of it—all 100 percent.

Christian stewardship begins with God's love, affirms God's ownership, and then celebrates God's partnership. There is nothing we do by ourselves. The apostle Paul reminded the church at Corinth that we are coworkers with God (1 Corinthians 3:9). There is nothing God calls us to do that God has not already provided us with the resources to accomplish.

Does your church do stewardship surveys? Many churches use such a survey as part of the finance campaign. It almost gives the message that a person can give money or time. The problem is that a survey begins at the wrong point: What can you do for the church? Stewardship begins not with what you can do for the church but with the gifts you have and how the church can assist you in putting your gifts to work for God's kingdom. Do you have members in your church who will say yes to anything? Do you have members who have taken on more than one job in the church and are not doing well in any of them? Do you have members who constantly say no when you ask them to do something? Maybe we have focused too much on what the church needs and not enough on how God is calling people into ministry.

Like most churches, Aldersgate always puts people on the finance committee if they have any finance background. Bob was the president of a local bank, so he was put on the finance committee as soon as he joined the church. He attended almost every meeting, but he rarely had anything to offer. One Sunday the pastor and Sunday school superintendent discovered that the first grade class did not have a teacher. Everyone they asked was busy, so they decided that the next person who came into the church would be placed in that classroom of first graders. Bob, who was the first one through the door, went willingly into the classroom. Fifteen minutes later the pastor and Sunday school superintendent felt guilty about what they had done. They looked in expecting to see young children running around the room and Bob tied up in extension cords in the middle of the floor. Well, Bob *was* on the floor; but so were all the children, who were listening intently to what Bob was telling them about Jesus. Bob's skills in his job were in money management. His gifts for ministry were in communicating to young children the love of God.

How often do we ask people to do the wrong thing? How often do we fill positions because there is a position to be filled on a nomination report? Stewardship understands that everyone is in a partnership with God, a partnership in which God provides the gifts for ministry. In a time when people are struggling to find their place in life, God's gifts for ministry, God's invitation to be in partnership, provide a clue of what life is about for each individual.

How Will You Define Stewardship?

1. Write down words you think are important in understanding stewardship.

2. Now talk about those words with someone else. Find out what words other people suggest when they hear the word *stewardship*.

3. Read the stewardship definitions on page 35. Highlight key words and phrases.

4. Discuss with someone else how those words and phrases make you feel about your stewardship.

5. Write your own brief definition of *stewardship*.

Stewardship Definitions

Stewardship is that for which I am responsible to God for my fellow-men.

(Reprinted from *A Theology for Christian Stewardship*, by T. A. Kantonen. © 1956 Muhlenberg Press. Used by permission of Augsburg Fortress.)

[Stewardship is] what I do after I have said, "I believe."

(Reprinted from *A Theology for Christian Stewardship*, by T. A. Kantonen, page 90. © 1956 Muhlenberg Press. Used by permission of Augsburg Fortress.)

Stewardship is always to allow faith to get loose and live itself out in the world.

(Thomas C. Rieke, Network for Charitable Giving, Oakland, CA 94621.)

Stewardship is the name we give to the practiced expressions of our faith.

(Thomas C. Rieke, Network for Charitable Giving, Oakland, CA 94621.)

Moving From Definition to Change

When we change our definition of stewardship to focus on the individual rather than on what the individual can do or can give, our ministries of stewardship change from finance campaigns to how to assist stewards to become transformed disciples. What can we do to begin making a difference in our churches? We can begin by

- focusing more attention on the meanings of stewardship;
- preaching more actively about stewardship;
- helping...members connect their faith to their work;
- responding to the pressures and anxieties that grow out of contemporary jobs and careers;
- rediscovering the churches' prophetic voice on matters of money and materialism.

(*The Crisis in the Churches: Spiritual Malaise, Fiscal Woe,* by Robert Wuthnow, page 12. © 1997 by Robert Wuthnow. Used by permission of Oxford University Press.)

The Tithe

One of the biblical standards regarding giving is the tithe. Any pretense of developing a theology of development or theological foundation for financial stewardship without considering the tithe is looking only at a partial theology. Tithing changes the focus of the giver. In some places it is referred to as the minimum standard of giving. But even more, it is a confession of faith, an act of worship, an act of dependence on God. With almost everything else we do in life, we point to our own control and success. However, in giving—especially in tithing—we turn to God in an act of praise, confession, and thanksgiving.

The tithe is a concept that is often talked about without any real understanding of its origins or importance in the role of a disciple. The tithe is an affirmation that God is the owner. It is more than paying God; it is an act of worship. I like to talk about sacramental giving, which is giving as an act of praise and worship.

The tithe did not originate with Jesus. Though Jesus said almost nothing about the tithe, he spoke frequently about money and possessions. One-third of Jesus' thirty-nine parables are about money, and there are many other teachings as well.

The tithe as a concept predates even the Bible. Long before the Old Testament, the Babylonians and Egyptians dedicated one-tenth to their gods. Why not one-eighth instead of one-tenth? In Egyptian numerology, ten was a sacred number with magical or mystical qualities. Although the concept of the tithe as one-tenth was not new, the Israelites (the early Jews) refined the concept. They clarified it and set it up as spiritually important for God's people.

There is no one concept of tithing in the Old Testament. It is almost as if the idea has gone through stages of development. As such, it often looks as if there are many tithes. In the earliest stages of their development as a community of faith, the Israelites were instructed to bring forth the first fruits of their labor (Exodus 22:29-30). They had a simple life as agricultural people living off the land. From the land would come their offering to God. It was an acknowledgment that all they had came from God. It reminds me of the hymn "We Give Thee But Thine Own," by William W. How, in *The Book of Hymns: Official Hymnal of The United Methodist Church* (The United Methodist Publishing House, 1964; page 181).

> We give thee but thine own,
> Whate'er the gift may be:
> All that we have is thine alone,
> A trust, O Lord, from thee.

Giving is an act of praise and worship. Could we learn something from this lesson?

Another stage in the development of the tithe came when the Israelites ended their pilgrimage and settled down as home owners. They erected more shrines and altars for local sacrifices. Then in the seventh century, when the Book of the Law (which we know as the Book of Deuteronomy) was found in the Temple in Jerusalem, King Josiah demanded that all the pagan shrines be destroyed. He also demanded that the commandments of the Lord found in the Book of the Law be kept (2 Kings 23:1-15), including the law that all offerings come only to the Temple in Jerusalem (Deuteronomy 12:11-14). Every third year they were to give another tithe to benefit local charitable purposes, such as caring for the widows and orphans (Deuteronomy 14:28-29).

Another stage in the development of the tithe came as the Temple in Jerusalem became the center of all religious activity. The members of the tribe of Levi, who were the caretakers of that Temple, were instructed to bring their tithe to support the Temple (Numbers 18:21).

In many ways, it looks as if the Old Testament talks about not one tithe but three tithes:

1. The first tithe is a standard of giving (Leviticus 27:30).
2. The second tithe is an act of thanksgiving (Deuteronomy 12:5-7).
3. The third tithe is a special tithe every third year for widows and orphans (Deuteronomy 14:28-29).

When you consider the first two tithes as 10 percent each and the third tithe as $3^1/_3$ percent per year over the three-year period, it looks like it is $23^1/_3$ percent per year. It sounds too legalistic, doesn't it?

That is where the New Testament comes in. It says little about the tithe because it assumes that tithing is an accepted fact, a minimum standard of giving. Jesus and the early church leaders go beyond the requirements of the law. The New Testament teaching is what is often referred to today as proportionate giving. The teachings fall into three basic categories:

1. Give regularly (1 Corinthians 16:2).
2. Give sacrificially (Luke 21:3-4).
3. Give joyfully (2 Corinthians 9:7).

Tithing is not about money; it is about being a partner with God.

John Wesley, an early leader of the Methodist movement, had many things to say about giving. One of his sermons, "The Use of Money" (Sermon 50), has popularly been summarized with the words: "Earn all you can. Save all you can. Give all you can." In the simplicity of John Wesley's words is a strong message.

1. Earn all you can—Do what you must to earn a good living. Make sure that all you do is seen as God's work. Give all you can to your work.
2. Save all you can—Now this is not as it seems. John Wesley had the gift of simplicity, so he lived on little. Of course, he had many people taking care of him wherever he went, just as Jesus did. He suggests that you spend only what you need. His guidance here is not so much about saving as it is about how we spend. Live frugally. I like the word *frugal.* One definition says that being frugal means using all that you have, fully.
3. Give all you can—This is sound advice. As stewards, we have so that we may give. To do any less is to rob God (Malachi 3:8).

Good Shepherd Church made stewardship education a vital part of their comprehensive plan. The following are the five categories they decided to use to guide stewardship education in their church. The emphases for each of the categories are listed, along with the primary resources that will be used in that phase of the stewardship education. (Ordering information for the primary resources is on pages 108–9.)

Our Ministry of Stewardship

Goal: To help people become giving stewards

1. The Giving Steward
Emphases
- Tithing, or proportional giving
- Believe people want to give; provide opportunities
- Provide giving models
- Involve leadership
  - storytelling
  - personal witnessing

Primary Resource
- *Stewardship: A Rainbow of Possibility,* by Donald Joiner.

2. The Gifted Steward
Emphases
- Search for meaning equals gifts for ministry
- Gifts versus time and talents
- Volunteer coordinator

Primary Resource
- *Gifts Discovery Workshop,* by Herb Mather.

3. The Personal Steward
Emphases
- Values set the agenda
- Personal financial management
- Wills and estate planning
- Endowment program
- Memorial opportunities

Primary Resource
- *Christians and Money: A Guide to Personal Finance,* by Donald W. Joiner (Nashville: Discipleship Resources, 1991).

4. The Church as Steward

Emphases

- Vision for ministry
- Fund campaign
- Leaders as stewards
- Worship as education

Primary Resources

- *Don't Shoot the Horse ('Til You Know How to Drive the Tractor): Moving From Annual Fund Raising to a Life of Giving,* by Herb Mather (Nashville: Discipleship Resources, 1994).
- *Get Well! Stay Well! Prescriptions for a Financially Healthy Congregation,* by Wayne C. Barrett (Nashville: Discipleship Resources, 1997).
- *Revolutionizing Christian Stewardship for the 21st Century: Lessons From Copernicus,* by Dan R. Dick (Nashville: Discipleship Resources, 1997).
- *The Church Finance Idea Book,* by Wayne C. Barrett (Nashville: Discipleship Resources, 1989).

5. The Public as Steward

Emphases

- Environment
- Vocation
- Mission experiences

Chapter Four

Developing Christian Philanthropists

Sally and John have been long-time supporters of St. Stephen's Church. Sally is involved with a small group that prepares the sanctuary for Sunday services. John is an active trustee who takes pride in how the physical facilities of the church look, both inside and out. He says that "a cared-for building and grounds show people that the church cares for them too." Sally and John love their church. Seventeen years ago they rarely went to worship and seldom gave more than $5 at a time. Today, they tithe 15 percent of their income to the church and are active in many areas of the church's life. Sally and John have become Christian philanthropists. What made the difference?

Contrast Sally and John to Bill and Fran. Fran is on the church board. Bill goes to worship with Fran on a regular basis (about once a month). When the church asks, they give $20 or so, but have no great need to give beyond that. Why is there such a difference in people within the same church? How can a church have more Sallys and Johns? Can a church do anything to move Bill and Fran, and the large number of other people like them in a church, to be better givers?

One task of the stewardship ministries of the church is to assist Christians to become givers. Note, however, that there is a difference between getting people to give and assisting people to become givers. Bill and Fran gave when they were asked. When stewardship ministries focus on bills and budgets, we invite people to give to support those budgets. When the church has a need, these people give. Beyond that, they find other places to spend their money. Over the years the church has taught people to support the church, rather than to be givers. Long-time members and older members of the church will still give if there is a need. If there is no stated need, there is no motivation to give beyond a minimum. When they are gone who will support the church? When a church moves from fundraising to raising Christian philanthropists, like Sally and John, something happens in the life of the membership, and the financial health of the church reaps significant rewards.

The apostle Paul describes, in his second letter to the church at Corinth, what it means to be a Christian philanthropist:

> We want you to know, brothers and sisters, about the grace of God that has been granted to the churches of Macedonia; for during a severe ordeal of affliction, their abundant joy and their extreme poverty have overflowed in a wealth of generosity on their part. For, as I can testify, they voluntarily gave according to their means, and even beyond their means, begging us earnestly for the privilege of sharing in this ministry to the saints—and this, not merely as we expected; they gave themselves first to the Lord and, by the will of God, to us, so that we might urge Titus that, as he had already made a beginning, so he should also complete this generous undertaking among you. Now as you excel in everything—in faith, in speech, in knowledge, in utmost eagerness, and in our love for you—so we want you to excel also in this generous undertaking. (2 Corinthians 8:1-7)

The church at Corinth had gone through a great deal of turmoil and in-fighting, primarily about the conditions of membership as a Christian in the church. Paul writes that it is time to forget all that and be drawn back into the work of ministry. To complete their healing, the Corinthians need to learn the blessings of giving. To illustrate, Paul points to the churches of Macedonia, including the churches at Philippi, Beroea, and Thessalonica. These churches were among the poorest of the Roman colonies; yet in their poverty they gave. They not only gave, but they gave a fabulous fortune. Paul says they gave not merely according to their means: They gave not just what was expected of them, but they gave beyond all measures of expectation. And they did it on their own.

The message of these verses is not about money but about disciple-ship. The message is that this liberality in giving is nothing but a spiritual miracle. How is the giving in your church and in your life? What we need today is nothing short of a spiritual miracle in giving. When we assist people to become Christian philanthropists, that spiritual miracle happens.

Remember that although the word *philanthropist* often generates images of a person who has given a large amount of money, being a philanthropist is really not about the amount of money someone gives. What matters is the motivation one has for giving. Dictionaries define philanthropists as people who have a desire to help humanity. News accounts of the first billion-dollar gift to charity made headlines. These accounts focused on this amazing gift. At the same time, one page of another magazine article listed what is happening every day: $57 million dollars was given by a well-known foundation; $22 million was donated by a publisher for a journalism school; and a hospital in Maryland was well on the way to its $100 million campaign goal.

Then there was Matt and Sue, who started tithing when they earned $20 a week and continued when they were making more than $80,000 a year. They continued even into retirement, when they began to discover new ways of giving.

Christian stewardship begins not with an inventory of what we have, but from a recognition of whose we are. We are children of God, blessed by an overabundance of grace. "For God so loved the world [that's us] that he gave his only Son, so that everyone who believes in him may not perish but may have eternal life" (John 3:16). Our giving is a spiritual miracle, because of what God has done for us in Jesus Christ. Doesn't that excite you?

Jesus told the story of a widow and her giving. (I sometimes refer to this story as the steward's mite.) She gave what she had, not because of some publicity, but because something inside her said she could do no other. This is the story of an early philanthropist.

Elizabeth, who lived only on her Social Security income in retirement, discovered that she could give her home to the church. Harry tithed not only his earnings but also the increase in his annual net worth. The youth of St. John's Church consistently give one-third of their earnings to mission. Hope New Paradigm Church is committed to give 43 percent of this year's budget to missions. These are stories of today's Christian philanthropists.

Neither Jesus nor the apostle Paul used the word *philanthropy,* but they talked about generous people who gave not from their wealth but from their faith. That is what makes them philanthropists.

The new paradigm of funding-ministry thinking will spend more time in understanding why people give and in giving birth to Christian philanthropists than in balancing the budget. A first step in building a culture where giving is motivated by being a Christian philanthropist is to understand that people want to give and that giving is possible.

The philosophical foundations in most congregations are still based on a 1950's philosophy that all people are broke and do not have anything to give. Wayne Barrett, in his article "Ministry in the Midst of Abundance" (*Celebrate Stewardship,* Volume 11, Number 4, November 1998), lays out the case for why the church needs to move away from an operational style of scarcity and move with the flow of abundance in our current culture.

1. **Americans are getting richer.** There is a growing cadre of wealth in America. In 1950, wealth was defined as a household with an income of $17,000. One in 50,000 households in 1950 met this definition. By 1990, the definition of wealthy was a household with an income of $100,000. One in twenty-five households had achieved this fame. By the year 2000, this definition had increased to a household income of $135,000, and one in seventeen households had achieved this level of income.

2. **The people who are getting richer belong to our churches.** Those who control the most money in America are over age 55. These people make up 21 percent of the population, but they control 80 percent of the wealth. These are the people who populate our churches.

3. **Almost every congregation can tap this new source of wealth.** If we focus giving on what the church needs, we limit the faithful expression of our members. When we limit giving to earned income, we limit the amount of a person's response. (See Chapter Seven, on pages 75–94, for more about giving beyond the budget.)

When you believe that people want to give and can give more than they do, the next step in building a climate for giving is to teach people the biblical models for giving. One of the major themes of the Bible is that life is a trust from God. In 1 Timothy 6:20, the apostle Paul warns his young protégé: "Guard what has been entrusted to you." Every trust carries with it a responsibility that is part of the covenant: God will be our God, will provide, care for us, and most of all love us. What is expected of us in return? One of our responsibilities is to give God our offering, our praise, our tithe in partnership with God. Although this responsibility is about giving, it is not just about money. It is about our relationship to God as expressed in this one way, giving.

What kind of guidance can we have regarding our stewardship as givers? The first place we should go for guidance is the Bible. Some of these points I have referred to earlier, but I want to emphasize them again in the context of our response to God's love and of our being a giver.

1. Everything is God's; I am not an owner but a steward.
2. Everything I have, as great or little as it is, God expects me to use to fulfill my partnership with God (Luke 12:13-21, parable of the rich fool).
3. God will keep me accountable for this trust (Matthew 25:14-30, parable of the talents).
4. God expects me to be a giver or, more appropriately, a steward (Luke 12:34: "For where your treasure is, there your heart will be also"—not the other way around).

A step in building such a culture of giving is to understand why people give. Why do you give? How do you calculate what you will give? My giving—and Paul says the giving of the Macedonians—is not motivated by what the church needs, which limits giving to a particular need or amount. Nor is it motivated by what I (or the Macedonians) have. It is motivated by something deeper. For me, faithful giving is an act of Christian discipleship.

When we open our hearts to the astounding message of what God has done, the miracle engulfs us. I read a story not long ago about a guest minister who when the time for the offering came, led the prayer for the offering. He prayed passionately, fervently, and convincingly that God would lead the people to see their offering as an expression of faithfulness, discipleship, and love of God. In the congregation sat a woman who literally had nothing to give. When the plate finally came to her, she looked at it for a moment. She slowly rose from her seat in the pew, stepped into the aisle, and quietly put the plate on the floor. Then, in a humble and beautiful act of devotion, she simply stepped into the plate.

Jesus said, "Where your treasure is, there your heart will be also," not the other way around. Giving is a sign of what we truly value. Paul says, "They gave themselves first." Can we help people decide what to give? Some people have a gift for giving that comes naturally, but the majority of people do not have such a gift. When three two-year-old children are playing in a room of toys, do they share? Or is David in the corner with as many of the toys as he can gather? Most people must be taught to be givers. Many Christians want to give, but the climate or culture has not been created for them to become givers. They do not know when to give or how often, let alone what to give.

Why do people give? Here is a list of some of the most common reasons people give:
• They want to express gratitude to God.
• It is a biblical mandate.
• They like what is happening at the church.

- They are looking to heaven (buying their way in).
- They want something for their children (or grandchildren).
- It is the way they were taught.
- It gives them power and control.
- It is a tax deduction.

The important thing to remember is that people give for many different reasons. Because you give for a certain reason (you like the choir) does not mean that someone else will be motivated to give for the same reason. You cannot make a person be a giver, but you can create the climate in which giving is learned, shared, and celebrated.

When you understand what motivates people to give, you can design a plan or strategy for your church. Here is a list of questions you might ask to determine which people are most likely to give:
- Were they part of a giving family?
- Did they come from another church, and did it teach giving?
- What is important to them?
- What is their spiritual maturity?
- What is their present financial situation?
- How do they feel about your church?

Spend some time asking people in your church why they give. To get helpful information, begin with people who are givers. Bring together a small group of your most faithful givers. Choose some because they are your top givers. Choose others because their giving is an indication of something deeper in their faith. Read 2 Corinthians 8 together; then ask them why they give. Have some of these Christian philanthropists tell their story of giving during the announcement time in worship. Have others write for your newsletter a small article about their decision to give. Support these people in their giving, and let them know at least twice a year that their faithful response is a shining example that is appreciated.

One finance campaign is designed around classes of people and their giving. Too often we try to get the inactive members to give like some of the best givers. It is not going to happen. Whatever message we give them about giving will fall on deaf ears. Have members who are generous givers (according to Paul's definition) write to those who are almost there, but not quite. Have them tell where they are in their giving and invite the receivers to increase their giving.

Ron and Sherry are not tithers. They feel the urge to tithe, but it seems like a big jump from 2 to 10 percent. They told others that they will increase their giving by 1 percent a year, at the least, to reach their goal. Ron and Sherry are more like most of the members of the church, but they do not know what to do. Have them write to people who give regularly to the church but are not among the top givers. They can invite others to join them in their journey of increasing by 1 percent.

Some people give to support missions, others to support the youth. Some give because of the minister, others because of the music. Some give because you ask, others because they like what is happening at the church. To create a climate in which giving can happen, tell the story of what the church is doing, how lives are touched, and when ministry is happening. This is an ongoing marketing task of the church. Under the offertory section of its bulletin each week, First Church puts a paragraph about how giving makes a difference. As an ongoing part of each Sunday service, People's Church has members witness about how lives are touched. People give to other people, to ministries, and to success.

What you believe about giving, what kind of giver you are, will affect the way people in your church give. What do you believe about giving? Here are some things I believe:

- Most people are not gifted givers.
- All Christians need to give.
- Giving must be sacrificial and sacramental to be called giving.
- For giving to be effective, we must take the responsibility of assisting people to be generous and cheerful givers.

Biblical Perspectives on Stewardship

Perspective	Key Passages	Theological Position
Creation	Genesis 1	God made it all. God made it good.
	1 Corinthians 3:21-23	Everything belongs to God.
Awaken	Genesis 2	We are to manage (have dominion), to tend the garden.
	Romans 8:18-25	The whole creation groans for redemption.
	John 10:10	Look at the original purpose to determine the desired end.
	Psalm 50:10-11	The abundant life.
Exodus (Liberation)	Genesis 3	Work (expulsion from the garden) (verse 23).
	Exodus (especially the manna story)	Follow the rules because God is gracious. There is enough.
Seek Justice	2 Corinthians 8:14-15	Use your wisdom in your freedom. Thanksgiving.
	Genesis 41–45	There is a sense of movement
	Genesis 28:20-22	in life—not fixed positions (process).

(Chart continued on page 50.)

Exile	Psalm 137	Live responsibly in the world
	Jeremiah (esp. 29)	far from God's intention.
	Ezekiel	Settle down, buy land, raise
		gardens, have families, teach
		about God.
Bring Hope	Second Isaiah	Live by faith and hope.
	Genesis 28:20-22	Living in spiritual exile.
	1 Peter (1:1-2, 17-21)	Stewards of the grace of God
	1 Peter 4:1-11	(see verses 2 and 7).
		What do you do when you have
		no corporate memory?
Grace	1 Corinthians 4:1-2	We are stewards of the Gospel
	John 3:16-17	first. God's gift is before all gifts.
	Romans 5:12-17	Free gift—abundance of grace.
	2 Corinthians 8	"Let me tell you about the grace
		of God."
	1 Peter 4:10	Good stewards of God's varied
		grace.
		Prevenient grace.
	Luke 24:13-35	Listen to the story/
	(Emmaeus)	share hospitality/
		share the story.

Written by Herb Mather. Copyright © the General Board of Discipleship, Nashville, Tennessee. Used by permission.

Chapter Five

How to Increase Giving in Your Church

Volunteer giving to churches, as we know it today, is a modern phenomenon. In agrarian times, when the product of people's work was in what they farmed and raised, what they produced was the source of their gifts to the church. During that time, churches often developed thanksgiving or harvest celebrations, in which people made gifts or commitments based on their harvest. Some of our church people still think in these terms. These harvest celebrations are probably the reason most churches still have fall campaigns. In the summer, pastors still receive bags and bushels of home-farmed products. Churches have tables of products to sell on Sunday mornings, often with the proceeds going to missions. When the American culture moved from an agrarian society to a more urban society and currency became the mode of trade, coins and money became the source of giving. In European and English society, the church was often supported by the state through taxes. Volunteer giving to charity was really not for the support of the church, but for ministry and mission. In North America, giving was often the task of a select group of people called stewards. These people were usually people of means in the community who were assigned an amount of money to raise for the church. With that responsibility, they either gave out of their own wealth or asked other people in the church and community to give toward their personal goal.

Just as the church has changed over the past fifty years—from a predominantly worship-centered ministry to one of small groups, outreach, and mission—so has the focus of financing the ministry of the church. Prior to 1950, most people in America lived from one paycheck to the next. They had few extras in their lives and rarely took vacations. Luxuries might mean a 10-cent movie or a piece of penny candy. Most people were paid in cash, in an envelope that sometimes made it home. Since giving to churches was in cash, envelopes and members' pledge numbers were important in order to know who gave what.

After World War II, life in America began to change. More and more people had money available after the bills were paid. Wages and payment of bills turned to bank drafts and personal checks. People began to have more time and money for vacations. Travel trailers and campgrounds became popular. More personal luxuries began to creep into people's lives. Giving to the church also changed, as checks were being put in offering plates instead of cash.

We are at the beginning of a new century, but most churches still face funding issues and giving as if we were still living in the 1950's.

- We talk about giving cash when there is a growing use of electronic transfer of funds.
- We talk about sacrificial giving when even the poor in America are wealthy according to world standards.
- We talk about living simply while living in the lap of luxury. (Even the smallest of automobiles has air conditioning and power windows and doors.)
- We talk about giving from earned income when personal assets are growing.

Maybe it is time to rethink the way we raise money in the church.

Do We Need a Commitment Program?

If the times are changing, a real question is, Do we need a program to allow people to make a financial commitment to the church? Before we answer, perhaps we need to answer a more basic question, Does making a financial commitment make a difference in giving?

Yes, it does. Study after study shows that people who make a commitment to the church generally will give more than people who make no commitment. When people are in church, they usually will give. When they are not there and have not made a commitment to give, they usually do not give. Wayne Barrett, a noted church finance expert, declares Barrett's Law: When they park it in the pew they plop it in the plate. (*The Church Finance Idea Book,* by Wayne C. Barrett, page 57. © 1989 by Discipleship Resources. Used by permission.)

> Congregations that use annual pledge drives and pledge cards have a higher level of giving.
>
> (Reproduced from *Money Matters: Personal Giving in American Churches,* by Dean R. Hoge, Charles E. Zech, Patrick H. McNamara, and Michael J. Donahue; page 82. © 1996 Westminster John Knox Press. Used by permission.)

> Congregations with high levels of giving realize that people who estimate their giving (pledge) do give more. Studies indicate that members who make estimates of their giving usually give at least 30 percent more than those who do not estimate.
>
> (*Generous People,* by Eugene Grimm; page 49. © 1992 by Abingdon Press. Used by permission.)

Your Church's Annual Campaign

One of the major advances in financing church budgets came not from the church but probably from the YMCA. The YMCA is often given credit for being the first to develop what churches have called an every-member commitment, which was an opportunity to spread the support to all members and friends of the church.

Some form of every-member visitation was the only finance campaign most local churches knew until the early 1970's. It often became a process of active members visiting less-active members to tell them what they should give. Canvassers were getting tired of it, but what else could they do?

The Circuit Rider, the Pony Express, and other variations came to the fore of church-funding campaigns in the early 1970's. They were less intrusive than every-member visitations. As society was slowly becoming less community oriented, as people's lives became busier, and as people had less and less to do with one another, a distribution program such as the Pony Express became popular. Packets of information and pledge cards were passed from one member's home to another. Little personal interaction took place, and for most people that was fine.

Year after year churches "rode the horse" until it died; then they dragged it for another five years. In recent years, churches find a campaign that works (such as Consecration Sunday) and use it until it dies also. Then, in frustration, they either mail letters (which usually do not work) or do nothing. Where is your church in its plans to run this year's finance campaign?

Which Fall Campaign?

Do you wait until early September every year to decide what to do for your church's annual finance campaign? Is there always a rush to decide? Do you turn to the same people every year to work on the campaign? Does your committee on finance assume that it must run the annual finance campaign every year?

Who should be responsible for running the finance campaign? The committee on finance is responsible for funding the church's ministry, but nothing says the committee cannot delegate the responsibility for the campaign. Delegation probably is a good idea, since no committee can effectively do more than two things at one time. Think of what is already expected of the committee on finance. I once listed thirteen tasks of this committee, including conducting the annual fund campaign, teaching tithing, recording and reporting funds, and educating people about wills and bequests. When an existing finance committee also tries to organize the annual finance campaign, the finance campaign is often short-changed. Therefore, it seems wiser to develop a specific team for this task. In fact, the best people for the campaign committee may be people who are not on the finance committee. Ask, "Who are the best people for the different tasks that need to be done?" Remember that if success is dependent on the number of people involved, then going outside the committee and involving other people will increase the program's chances of success.

Many funding programs are available. Which program is the best one for your church? Certain actions will be part of any program:

• mailings to inform and inspire the congregation;
• short lay messages during worship that focus on giving, membership, and faith;
• one or more (usually three or four) stewardship sermons;
• articles and information about the plans in a newsletter or bulletin.

If yours is like many committees, you review a lot of options. Then you do what you have done in the past, even if it did not work well. A healthier way to plan the annual finance campaign is to follow the Cycle Theory of planning. Using it, you can plan the next three years; then you let the cycle begin again for another three years.

The Cycle Theory recognizes that the more consecutive times a local congregation uses a particular financial commitment program, the less effective it is. It is easiest for the leadership of the church to do the same thing they did last year; however, each program, each type of communication, each type of message will get only certain people or segments of your congregation to respond. Using the same program year after year will tend to reach the same people again and again. What about those people you are missing? The Cycle Theory suggests that local congregations get on a cycle of different programs. Each of the following groups of campaigns have different purposes, involve people differently, and have varying degrees of success. Under each grouping is a list of resources. Decide the type of campaign you need; then choose a program. (Ordering information for the resources is on pages 108–9.)

Year One: Celebration Sunday
Purpose: To use the Sunday morning worship service as a time to involve people in making financial commitments

The focus of Celebration Sunday is to use the time in worship to help people grow in their understanding of and commitment to the ministry of your church. But be careful. In most churches, only one-fourth to one-third of the members will be in church on any given Sunday. Just because you gave a beautiful message or told some vital information on one Sunday, do not think that all the members heard it. Tell it often and tell it in different ways.

Resources
- *Celebration Sunday* (LeWay Resources).
- *Consecration Sunday* (Cokesbury).
- *In the Light of God's Grace* (Resource Services, Inc.).
- "Seeking Something Better," in *The Abingdon Guide to Funding Ministry,* Volume 2 (Cokesbury).

Year Two: One-on-One Communication

Purpose: To present and market the church's story through home groups, phone calls, small groups, visitations, dinners (if there is room for dialogue)

The focus of a one-on-one communication program is to let people in on your secret: This church is an exciting and vital place in which ministry and mission happen. This type of program provides a time to talk to people, to present your story of ministry on as personal a basis as you can, even if it is in a group. The communication may be done by phoning, visiting homes, or meeting in groups at the church. To make this method work best, find several ways to reach different people.

Resources

- *Called to Serve* (LeWay Resources).
- "Stewardship Fair," in *The Abingdon Guide to Funding Ministry,* Volume 1 (Cokesbury).

Year Three: Quick-and-Easy Programs

Purpose: To provide opportunities for as many people as possible, with as little personal contact as possible, to make financial commitments

Quick-and-easy programs use more impersonal ways to communicate with members than other programs. Direct mailing or circulating a packet among homes are some ways you can tell about the possibility of giving. The focus of this program is getting the commitment card out to people and back again in the easiest way possible. This program works for a large group of people who are already committed to the church. It does little to increase giving. (Note: My title for this kind of program may not be fair, but it explains the reduced time involvement required of the committee members.)

Resources

- *Pony Express* (Resource Services, Inc.).
- *Special Delivery* (LeWay Resources).
- *The Joy of Belonging* (Resource Services, Inc.).
- *The Joy of Discovery* (Resource Services, Inc.).
- *The Quill* (Church Fund Raising Services).

Whatever program you use, remember that the more you use the same program in successive years, the less effective it will be and the smaller group of people it will reach. If, however, you choose one of the above categories of programs each year (or use the same program for a maximum of two successive years), you will have a three-year cycle of fundraising campaigns and will not have to spend much time deciding which program to use. Follow the cycle and spend more time telling your story, involving more people, and reaching members with the good news of your ministry.

Choosing a Chairperson

Do you have trouble recruiting a chairperson for the annual campaign? Do you just pass the position around the finance or stewardship committee, even if the person you select does not want the job, or is the wrong person for the job? That is how most congregations do it.

The problem in most churches is that along with an invitation to take a position comes the unspoken invitation to keep doing that same job until a successor is recruited (which could be years, and years, and years). You need the most capable person available to lead your annual finance program. With the Cycle Theory, you know a year in advance which program you will have next year. Why not recruit a different general chairperson for each year of the cycle?

Recruit the chairperson for next year's annual finance campaign just before you begin this year's program, or at least as soon as this year's program is completed. He or she will not have to attend any meetings until next year. Provide that person with the program resources and supporting material about funding ministry in general. (A number of excellent resources are available from Discipleship Resources. Call 800-685-4370 or visit the Internet bookstore at www.discipleshipresources.org.) The new chairperson can spend the year studying the plan, reading the supporting material, deciding which people would be best for each job, and planning for the next campaign.

Committees may be tempted to rush through the planning steps; however, the more time spent in planning, the better chance the program has of succeeding. Encourage the chairperson to pray, read the materials, think through the program, meet with the pastor, and begin identifying the right people to assist in a successful program.

Let the chairperson know that his or her position is a one-year commitment. Do not make the mistake of giving people too many jobs. The chairperson for the finance campaign should have only that job for the year. The actual work will take about three months (but not much less). The chairperson may plan to meet occasionally with the finance committee to check the progress of the planning.

Recruit someone else to run the annual finance campaign the next year. Give this year's chairperson a break. He or she might want to be a consultant to the new group, or may prefer to stay out of it altogether since it will be a different program. But no matter what, when you select the chairperson for next year's program this year, you are always a year ahead on your plan.

When Is the Right Time?

"Rev. Dobbs, we have a dilemma!" Pattie Spears, chairperson of the committee on finance, explained to the pastor that the finance committee had been in a deadlock the night before. For three meetings now they had talked about what to do about the annual finance campaign this fall, without coming to any conclusions.

"Every year it's the same old thing," she explained. "We never start thinking about the annual need to raise the finances until after Labor Day. Then we feel like we are in a major rush to think of something to do and get it organized and over with by Thanksgiving. Last night we couldn't even find someone who would chair the committee. Everyone is so busy with other things that no one has the time to organize this year's finance campaign. What are we going to do?"

This scenario is a growing phenomenon in many congregations. It seems as if the church year starts in September with a major rush to get programs started, to organize bazaars and chicken barbecues, to recruit teachers, to get Christian education programs up and running, and to get committees and task forces thinking about the upcoming year. In addition, fall community sports begin then.

Is there a better time of the year to hold the finance campaign? Do we have to do it in the fall? In one seminar where I suggested that it could be done at a different time of the year, I said, "Someplace in the Old Testament it says that all churches must run their finance campaigns in the fall." Someone in the back of the room said, "It's in Second Hezekiah." I said, "No. It's more like Second Hesitation."

Is the fall the best time of the year to run your church's annual finance campaign? It depends. In a growing number of churches, the fall is becoming the most difficult time to do such a program. Not only is the church and community busy organizing and running things, but every community, educational, and charitable organization you can think of is asking for money. One fall evening when I was home alone, no less than six children and youth came to my door seeking contributions (actually, trying to sell me something) for elementary-school projects, Cub Scouts, band boosters, little league football. At work there was the annual fall push to pledge to a certain community organization. By the time the church gets around to asking me for my annual commitment, I am given out.

Gilson Miller's skit "The Appeal" (*The Abingdon Guide to Funding Ministry: An Innovative Sourcebook for Church Leaders,* Volume 1; Abingdon Press, 1995; pages 92–93) is about this same problem. A man had been looking forward to spending a Saturday afternoon at home alone watching his favorite team play the top contender in football. He planned the day out carefully. He placed his favorite chair in front of the television. On the table next to his chair, he placed the remote control (with new batteries), a bowl of popcorn, and his favorite six-pack of soft drinks. He was ready when the game began; but each time there was a hot play in the game, someone came to the door asking him to give money or to buy something. The last knock on the door came from a team of people from the church. The man was so upset that he ripped off his shirt and threw it at them, saying something like, "All I have left is the shirt off my back!" How many people in your church feel the same way about your finance campaign?

So, when is the best time to have your church's annual finance campaign? Any time it works. Free up your thinking and your plans. There is no right time for every church, but every church has its right time. Each church and community is different. Holding a fall finance campaign where my mother lives in Florida would be disastrous because people do not start coming back to her community, at least not in significant numbers, until after the holidays. January or early February may be better in that community than the fall. Yet, in a small community in northern Michigan, a January campaign may be the absolute worst time (people are gone and snow covers everything). Waiting until the fall in a resort community (after all the summer support has left) would be too late. However, in an agricultural community it may be just the right time. The right time to lead your church into making financial commitments is

- **When your church has something to shout and celebrate about its ministry.** The annual finance campaign is not about money and budgets. It is about commitment to the vision of the church in ministry and mission. Each church is appointed by God to accomplish a specific partnership with God in its community of faith. What is your church's vision of that ministry? It does not always take money to do ministry. Find out what your church is doing; then tell that story whenever you can.

- **When people feel good about your church.** The time for a commitment to the ministry of the church is when people know what that ministry is all about and feel good about it. The annual finance campaign is, after all, a type of marketing campaign: helping people know about, be enthusiastic about, and ready to make a commitment to the ministry of God through a particular church. One of the best ways to help people feel good is to tell stories that help members picture the church in action. That is not a budget, nor is it a list of programs and plans. People want to know the results of your church's ministry. What are some of the stories of the results of ministry in your church?

- **When people feel good about money in their life and giving.** People decide how much to give not according to how much money they have but on the basis of how they feel about money in their life. I felt great about the results of one campaign for which I had leadership. The amount contributed was more than the goal, and I knew it was because of my outstanding leadership—until I discovered that the major employer in that community had given out bonus checks on the Friday prior to the campaign. How people feel about money, not how much they have, makes a difference. When do the members of your church feel the best about money in their life? In one church I suggested they wait a while before conducting their campaign. They were ready to have Commitment Sunday the second Sunday in October. Then the announcement of a pastoral change that was effective September 1 was made. I suggested that they wait until early December for Commitment Sunday. Some thought people would be spent out in December because of Christmas. However, we discovered that people were in a giving mood in December. They had no idea how much they had spent until the bills came in January.
- **When you have the time to do it adequately.** The longer you plan—the more time that is spent organizing, involving, and telling the story of your church—the better your results will be. Most campaigns take about six to eight weeks of preparation, four intense weeks of campaigning, and two to four weeks of follow-up. Remember that the campaign is about ministry and mission and vision, not about facts and figures and budgets. It is really a marketing campaign, and it takes time to tell and hear the story.

Whenever I mention a different time of the year for the annual campaign, I always get a few "yes, buts." The biggest hesitancy comes from treasurers. "This sounds good, but what do I do about my reporting? All my reporting is on an annual basis." One of the first things a church needs to get away from is the idea of an annual budget. There is no such thing as an annual budget. Well, not really. What you really have are monthly budgets. Every month is different: What you need to spend and what you get for income is not the same each month. Plan out your income and expense needs on a monthly basis. Then you can take any twelve-month period (or any period of time: 6 months, 18 months) and make that your budget time.

Software programs can be configured without too much work to reflect your time period. If you see things on a monthly basis, you can take the twelve months the general church needs for reporting and add up what they need. Reporting to members on an annual basis for their income tax returns can be done simply by adding up the twelve months of a calendar year and sending a letter reporting their giving.

When is the best time for your church's annual finance campaign? Only you and the other leaders in your church can know that. Instead of always having the campaign at the same time of the year, try to understand the uniqueness of your congregation. Be open to the idea that when you have always done it may not be the best time for your church. Each congregation is different.

Chapter Six

The Disappearing Annual Campaign

At the great fund-raising churches in America, stewardship is a perpetual theme, not a special campaign.

(*How to Increase Giving in Your Church,* by George Barna, page 107. © 1997 by George Barna. Used by permission of Regal Books, Ventura, CA 93003.)

For many years the primary means of funding a church's ministry has been the annual stewardship campaign. Today, more and more churches are finding that this type of campaign, which has almost nothing to do with stewardship but more to do with getting enough money to finance the budget, is less and less effective. Although most churches will still need to conduct annual finance campaigns, the growing trend in American churches is to eliminate the finance campaign as a once-a-year activity. Churches are moving to a year-round system not of raising money but of giving birth to Christian philanthropists who are intentional about giving to, through, and beyond their local congregations.

In Chapter 5, I made a case for the annual campaign. Why am I now trying to make a case for abandoning the annual campaign? Annual campaigns can be a precious project for some churches, but my recent studies of per-member giving show that more than one-half of the congregations surveyed did nothing for a finance campaign last year. Many congregations have abandoned the annual campaign because it is no longer an effective program for them. If there is no annual campaign, what is a church to do?

I am not saying that every church should eliminate the annual finance campaign, but I am saying that they should expand the scope of the annual campaign to a year-round objective of giving birth to Christian philanthropists and funding ministry. Aside from the particulars of running an annual campaign, what does an effective finance campaign do?

1. It makes a case for the ministry of the church.
2. It communicates that case to the membership.
3. It invites people to make a response.

The problem with most annual campaigns is that when the campaign is over, the committee disbands and the church forgets to do anything else. A campaign builds a person's knowledge, motivates commitment, and invites response. However, the more time that passes after the annual campaign has ended, the more people forget, the less motivated they are, and the more they wonder why they made such a commitment in the first place. The most effective campaign takes the above steps—making a case, communicating the case, and inviting response—and makes an annual activity into a year-round ministry.

In recent studies of churches across North America, I made the following discoveries:

- Churches that invite disciples to be stewards of all of life have financially healthier congregations.
- When members connect activity, program, and even worship to that church's mission and vision, then attendance, volunteering, and giving increase.
- People give when they are convinced there is something good happening with their giving. That message cannot be told only once a year during an annual campaign.
- What people put on their commitment card is not the most they will give to the church.
- People give to people, ministries, and results, not to budgets, statistical analyses of spending, and reports.
- Different people and demographic age groups (generations) listen, see, and hear the same information differently.

These studies point out why what we have done for so many years is no longer working. With this new way of thinking about funding ministry, church leaders will need to spend more time on developing comprehensive stewardship strategies that focus on giving birth to Christian philanthropists than on balancing the budget. They will need to spend more time on understanding why people give than on an annual finance campaign. They will need to learn that an effective finance campaign cannot be completed in a short eight- to twelve-week fall program, but it will need to be part of the church's year-round, comprehensive stewardship strategy. Let us consider some of the findings of studies about church giving.

Churches that invite disciples to be stewards of all of life have financially healthier congregations. Some churches announce with pride that whenever they need money, they get it. That money could be for a new piano (as in a recent church), a new roof, or a van to transport older members on their outings outside the church.

What are we creating when people give only when asked? Is that stewardship? Have we created a membership of people who are generous only if asked? What do they do the rest of the time? They give elsewhere. Gerry is an active member of her town's Samaritan Center, which provides resources for people in need. She not only volunteers but also contributes financially to their growing needs. When asked why she does not give more to the church, she responded in surprise, "You mean the church needs more?" Over the years the church has taught her that if they need more, they will ask. Since the church has not been asking, Gerry assumed the church had no needs. Churches have created a climate in which people give only when the church asks.

Churches that have created a climate of giving associated with needs have raised members who respond only to needs. Congregations that raise Christian philanthropists raise members who give because it feels good, it is the right thing to do, and they want to honor God. Congregations that focus on the financial needs of the church to inspire giving raise members who have done their part. Some members have even figured out what part is their fair share. Anything beyond that would take away from someone else's share.

When members connect activity, program, and even worship to that church's mission and vision, then attendance, volunteering, and giving increase. In a world where people are being besieged by charities, why would anyone want to give to your church? The reason is simple, and it is not because they believe in what you are doing more than what the next charity is doing. It is because they are giving out of a deep-felt response to what God has done, and is doing, with them in Jesus Christ.

Your church is the best representative of that transformation in their lives. They want others to experience what they are feeling.

Other charities tell about what they are doing and ask for financial support. Your church builds people who are transformed and invites them into a relationship of transforming others. The difference rests on helping people discover that transformation and their response to it. (We call that stewardship.) It takes time, patience, and perseverance for people to discover that transformation and to link it to the work of your church. When we give birth to disciples who are generous givers, or what this book has been calling Christian philanthropists, we find people giving, giving more often, and giving more. To them, giving is an act of faith rather than a response to needs.

It is not enough to expect people to come and give. When that is the climate, all kinds of excuses can be made for not giving: too busy, too strapped for cash, other things (such as my daughter's soccer team) take too much of my time. On the other hand, people who enjoy giving have a sense of what the church is doing. They believe that what the church is doing is right, that it is what God wants done, and that God wants them to be part of it.

Have members of your church decided to take some time off from leadership, or even from participating at all? They talk about being burned out, which has less to do with energy than with lack of vision and mission. A key to giving success is people knowing that the church has a mission, a vision of what God wants that church to do in ministry. Your church can connect people to the mission and vision of the church through

- stories of ministry told before the offering;
- articles in the newsletter or bulletin;
- inserts that come from the denomination's offices;
- information that connects mission and vision to actions taken at council or board meetings;
- pictures and articles in local newspapers about your church.

People give when they are convinced there is something good happening with their giving. That message cannot be told only once a year during an annual campaign. For many people in your church, it seems like their giving goes into a dark hole and never comes out. When members tell you they want to know where the money goes, they do not want a finance report of the line items of the budget. They want to know that their giving makes a difference. Find ways to tell stories of lives touched by the work of your church.

Remember Esther, the eight-year-old girl who thanked her congregation for the Bible she had received in her Sunday school class? "That is the only

Bible in our home," she told the congregation. Then she told about sitting on the couch with her mother and opening the Bible to the story of Zacchaeus. She said it was the first time she had heard that story, and she began to tell it to the congregation. Esther's story was an excellent way for the congregation to know how their giving is making a difference in people's lives.

Follow Trinity's example. Invite members and friends of the church to tell why the church's ministry is important to them. Kathy told about how important the church became to her when she suddenly became a single mom with three kids under nine to raise by herself. Her family was a thousand miles away. It was through the Bible class for women that she really found the support she needed—spiritually, emotionally, and actually—to raise those children. Pam's parents decided to move near her after Pam's dad had a heart attack. It was not just to be near their daughter, but to be part of the church that had supported them through the surgery and rehabilitation. When Jon stood up to tell about the youth retreat, I expected to hear stories of pillow fights and water balloons thrown from the balcony of the hotel. Instead, he told how he had discovered purpose to his life. He said that when they were studying baptism, he first discovered the meaning of grace. Find ways to connect your members with these stories of meaning and purpose because your church is in ministry.

What people put on their commitment card is not the most they will give to the church. If you assume that what is written on the card is all someone will give, as most church leaders do, then you will do nothing during the rest of the year to help people respond to the call of God in their lives. In truth, there is little relationship between what people put on their commitment card and giving reality.

Earning and giving have changed drastically over the years. Unfortunately, the church's thinking about giving has not changed much in the past fifty years. I remember when my dad received a cash envelope every Friday with his pay. He knew what he earned because he saw it in his cash envelope. He made his plans around that money. When it was gone, that was it. Today, with automatic deposits and automatic withdrawals, most people do not know what they are earning or how they will spend it. Giving is seldom based on any reality, but rather on how people are feeling about their church, their involvement, and their available income at the time of their commitment. For example, when we ask people in October to give according to their earned income, they give one response. If we ask them in April (around tax time) to estimate their earned income, they give a different answer. The response varies according to the time of year.

People respond better to year-round considerations of giving than to an annual commitment. Your success with an annual campaign may well depend on the circumstances of the givers' lives, or even on the status of the financial markets. If you have your campaign at the wrong time (and that time may be different for different people), you may not get the results you had hoped for.

Find ways to invite people to respond in their giving on a more regular basis. One church wrote to members during tax season to invite them to tithe their refund from the Internal Revenue Service. As one member explained, it was not money they had planned for anyway. Another church found that when their members went on vacation, giving decreased. To offset that reality, they gave members special vacation envelopes to use for their giving before they went on vacation. Their summertime giving increased 35 percent the first year.

Think outside the box. Over the past fifty years or so we have focused only on giving, through an offering plate on Sunday morning. I saw a cartoon that showed a modern church with an ATM machine in the foyer. I am not advocating an ATM in every church, but perhaps we have forgotten that the process of giving has grown. It may be time for us to provide additional ways for people to give.

If we believe that people give only what they put on their commitment card, we will not provide opportunities and possibilities of giving outside the offering plate. It is time to update our view of what, how, and when to give. Consider electronic transfer of funds on an automatic basis. My membership in the YMCA can be paid only on an automatic draft from my account to the Y's account each month. Some people will pay anything they can with a credit card, in order to get their points. Your church could allow people to give through their credit cards each month. Have you considered allowing people to give through your church's Web site, especially to special projects and missions?

Some churches are experimenting with shorter (less than a year) commitments. With a rapid-paced lifestyle, changing demands, and a mobile public, a three-month or six-month commitment may make sense. We once thought of long-range planning as three to five years, or longer. Today, people have trouble thinking beyond the next three months. For some people, a one-year campaign is a long time to commit. Know your congregation and understand that no one way works for everyone.

Think beyond the offering. Giving from earned income on a weekly basis is fast disappearing as the norm for giving. For many, their paycheck does not even pay for their ongoing wants. A report by Paul Schervish and John Havens estimates that between $41 trillion and $136 trillion will be passed from one generation to another in the next 55 years. Where will your church be in that vast transfer of assets?

People want to give more, but churches have provided opportunities for them to give only from what is left in their checkbooks. Solutions to giving desires can be found all through your members' finances. For example, I am learning about more people than ever giving from accumulated assets: stocks, bonds, and mutual funds.

People give to people, ministries, and results, not to budgets, statistical analyses of spending, and reports. The old way of financial reporting was to give each person a copy of the budget at the time of the annual campaign, to report weekly statistics in the bulletin, and to send quarterly statements to encourage people to catch up. Most people do not want, or understand, financial data. A mutual fund company recently conducted a survey to find out how well people read the company's prospectus (their financial story) that they are required to send. They discovered that most people threw them out without reading them. The prospectus did not influence many people to invest; however, what their friends said did. It is the same in the church. People do not care where the money is allocated. They care only that it is well-managed and makes a difference.

The budget is a necessary tool for the management of the church. The finance committee, the treasurer, and the church staff all need the budget for their management tasks. However, church members do not care about the budget. I learned this lesson well from Herb, the stewardship committee member who pointed out that some line items in the church budget were more than he had made in a year. He said, "I just want to know where it is going."

Create a program or narrative budget. Ask your committees to tell stories of where the funds for those line items are being spent. Instead of saying $11,000 is needed for music, tell about the seven choirs and the five pianos that need to be tuned for those choirs. Remind members about past performances, such as the special youth cantata last spring and the Christmas musical.

What kind of response does your church get from the quarterly statement you send out? Several years ago I wrote about my American Express Plan. I charge most of my travel expenses to a credit card. I think that American Express does the best job of communicating with me through the monthly statement. I began asking why we do not do a better job of communicating through the (usually) quarterly statement we send out from the church. Instead of sending just a statement of giving, why not use this mailing to communicate to the members about their giving and to invite them to give more? If we are sending these statements out on a regular basis anyway, why not include some other information? It would not cost much more. Use this mailing to express your appreciation for their giving.

People want to know that their giving is making a difference. To let them know it does, tell stories of where their money is going. One problem with announcements and stories we tell during worship is that it is heard only by those who attend. Repeat some of the stories that are told during your worship (like when Esther received the Bible) so that all can know. Even those who heard it in worship will be glad to hear it again.

One of the reasons people do not give more regularly is that they have been taught that they can give only if they come to church. Include with the statement of giving an envelope they can use to make an additional gift any time they want. Have the envelope addressed to the church so that it gets to the right place.

Different people and demographic age groups (generations) listen, see, and hear the same information differently. In this age of consumerism, at a time when marketing surveys and customer satisfaction are high on most companies' list of things to do, why is the church still trying to push one message and one way of doing things to all its members?

We have attempted to put all people in the church in one category. However, people think, behave, believe, and react differently from one another. To define one way (for example, a finance campaign) for people to interact with the transformation in their lives and to make decisions about what to do with their faithful giving response is to deny them a positive chance to respond.

Because different people give and respond to messages and invitations differently, we need to use many methods and ways of involving people in responding to the ministry of the church. Some people respond favorably to a written message; others respond to a fast-paced visual message. Some want to support the church buildings; others are more interested in whose lives are changed and how. Some are highly involved and give more; others are on the sidelines and fail to see how their giving is important or makes a difference. Some are analytical and will respond to budgets and statistical figures; others respond to stories of lives transformed and to ministry results.

In his book *The Church Finance Idea Book,* Wayne Barrett points to the fact that different people give for different reasons (Discipleship Resources, 1989). Dan Dick moves this concept further in his book *Revolutionizing Christian Stewardship for the 21st Century: Lessons From Copernicus* (Discipleship Resources, 1997).

First Church decided to take this concept and use it to replace their normal annual finance campaign. They believed that any one program they might use, or any one approach, would communicate to only a few people. Therefore, they decided to do a multilevel approach to their finance campaign. They divided their congregation into four categories of members (actives, supporters, attenders, less-than-actives); then they designed a way to communicate to each category in a different way. The following are the categories and methods they chose.

Actives are those who show up for most programs, give nearly every time you ask, hold leadership positions, and are in church nearly every Sunday. People who may not be leaders but are among the top 12 to 15 percent of the givers of the church also belong in this category, as do people whose giving is considered a tithe. (This includes people like the widow in Jesus' parable of the widow's mite.) These people believe in the work of the church and will respond to almost anything you do, as long as it is positive. They need to be affirmed and thanked. They need to know the vision and mission of the church and what part they are playing to facilitate God's ministry. Special leadership dinners and periodic thank-you notes go a long way in communicating to this audience. The largest increase in giving will almost always come from this group. This audience will know what tithing is and will give some effort to become faithful givers.

Supporters are those who participate in committees, attend on a regular basis (less than the actives, but more than the attenders), and respond when asked to give. They support the church, but are not always clear on what the church is doing or why the church is doing it. More than any other audience, this audience needs the newsletters, the stories of what the church is doing, and intentional processes in asking them to make a commitment. They will respond if asked, but they often do not volunteer either their time or their giving without being asked. Most finance campaign strategies will work on this audience. This group needs models such as a step-up chart (see page 72) to assist them in making a decision on what to give.

Step Up Your Giving

give $100 or more a week
give between $75 and $100 a week
give between $50 and $75 a week
give between $25 and $50 a week
give between $15 and $25 a week
give between $10 and $15 a week
give between $5 and $10 a week
give $5 or less a week

We invite you to discover where you are on this step-up chart and to go up one step in your giving.

An effective strategy in one church was having the actives write to the supporters to invite them to go up one step in their giving. Inviting this group to consider a 1-percent increase in their giving will find positive response.

Attenders are those whom you most likely will see only on Sundays and in worship. Even then, their attendance may be only two or three Sundays a month. They usually skim, but rarely read, the newsletter. They will often not make a pledge. They will respond to what is happening in worship, so it may be your only time to communicate with them. Because they will not be in worship every Sunday (after all, only one-third of an average church's members are in church on any given Sunday), you cannot rely on telling a message or story only once and getting through to every worshiper. Therefore, themes, processes, and invitations need to be handled on at least a monthly basis, in order to reach the bulk of this audience.

Less-than-actives are those who rarely (and those who never) give or attend church. In many ways, we have told these people that they cannot give to the church unless they come to worship. Because they do not attend regularly, churches often do not bother to give them envelopes, quarterly statements, or any other way to give or to know what is going on in the church. They do not read the newsletter. The only way to reach this audience is through active mailings at least three times a year. Give little attention in these mailings to asking for money, and make sure it does not look as if they are being targeted. The message to this audience is a public-relations message about what good the church is doing, how lives are being touched by the ministries of the church, and what an exciting place it is. Include a return envelope in the mailing, and in a postscript invite them to use the enclosed envelope if they want to make a gift through the church.

Do churches need an annual finance campaign? Some do, some do not. Research continues to show that churches that have a proactive finance campaign, where people are given a chance to make a financial commitment, have a higher per-member giving ratio than do churches that do nothing. Yet it is not the type of campaign that makes a difference; it is the attitude of the leaders and the approach that make the difference. When a church replaces its goal of increasing the budget with a goal of helping people make a faithful response, wonders will happen. The church will be on its way to giving birth to Christian philanthropists.

Chapter Seven

Beyond the Offering: Planned Giving and Your Church

Elizabeth, one of the sweetest and most supportive members of the church, went to a stewardship training event one spring. As a widow without children, she had plenty of time to go to all sorts of training events. She was a good giver to the church, considering the little income she had in retirement, but she felt bad that she could not give more. At the seminar she went to one workshop, and I went to another one. She was bubbling and excited that night on the way home. "You look radiant," I commented. "What did you learn tonight?" She explained that she wanted to do more for the church, but she had little extra income to give. She said she had learned that night that she could give her house to the church and still live in it until she died. She was happy she had found a way to give, to support her church, without limiting her meager financial resources. But before she could make this gift happen, she fell down the stairs and died. I vowed then to learn more about ways people can give, not to increase the resources of the church but to assist faithful Christians to accomplish their goal of giving.

A pastor from a neighboring community called and said that he was angry. I wondered what I had done. He explained that a member of the church had just given a large sum of money to the local college, but had never made a major gift of any kind to the church. In explaining his anger, he said, "When I asked why he had never made such a gift to the church, he responded, 'I didn't know I could.' "

Take a survey at your next church leaders meeting. Ask those who have a current will to raise their hands. Anywhere from one-third to one-half will raise their hands. Then ask those whose hands were raised to keep them raised if they have included the church in their will or estate plan. Ask the others why they did not include the church in their plans. The usual response will be, "I didn't know I could" or "It never entered my mind."

We are entering a time in the American culture of unprecedented wealth. One generation is in the process of passing on to the next generation a wealth that has been estimated at between $10 and $41 trillion. Sometimes the estimates are even higher. Will your church be a recipient of any of that transfer of wealth? Of all those people who have died in your church or community in the past three years, how many had gifts of estate transfers that came to your church?

There was a time in our society when the goal of a family was to earn all they could, save all they could, and pass on to their heirs all they could, so that their children's lives would be better. Today, with the people I talk to about the transfer of their wealth, the response is usually twofold: "My children have so much now that I don't know if I need to leave them much," and "I don't know if I want to leave them anything, because I don't like the way they are managing what they have now."

Giving from one's estate, both during one's lifetime and at death, is the fastest growing source of income to the church today. The annual increase of giving by bequests has been almost double that of the increase of giving from earned income.

The church has focused on giving only from earned income for far too long. As earned income is being drawn against for so much else in life, and as the amount of earned income available for discretionary choice (such as giving) decreases, the amount of church giving through the offering plate will be challenged. The Newtithing Group, a not-for-profit organization in northern California, points to giving from assets as the growing edge of funding. They estimate that Americans could give almost three times what they are giving and not affect their overall wealth. *Churches that fail to give attention to giving from one's assets will be lucky to survive in the future.*

Giving, as a response of one's stewardship in support of the ministries of the church, is changing. When our livelihood came from farming or raising cattle, Christians gave from their "first fruits." When we moved into a cash society, when people were paid in a cash envelope at the end of the week, Christians gave cash from earned income. As we moved into a check-driven society, churches were slow in providing ways for people to give through checks made out to the church. Now we are moving into a new economy with growing assets. *Churches that fail to give attention to giving from one's assets will be lucky to survive in the future.*

Rick told me in an e-mail the other day that he was frustrated. He had his stock broker transfer $5,000 of stocks from his account to the church. It made sense to him to make this gift, and it allowed him to give more to his church than he would have given to the capital campaign. He had paid $100 for the stock. If he sold the stock, he would receive only around $4,000 after paying federal and state taxes on the capital gain. If he gave it to the church, the church would benefit from the entire $5,000. When the church received the stock transfer, the treasurer sent it back to the broker and said the church could not accept it. Our leaders and members need to be educated about the new economy and the new way of giving. *Churches that fail to give attention to giving from one's assets will be lucky to survive in the future.*

Jill left the church a gift of 25 percent of the proceeds of her life insurance policy when she died. The church received a check from the insurance company two months after Jill's death, but they held onto the check for the next three months trying to figure out what to do with it. *Churches that fail to give attention to giving from one's assets will be lucky to survive in the future.*

When a church opens the doors of planned giving (giving from one's accumulation) at least five things will happen:

1. The church will receive increased gifts to fund various ministries.
2. Members will begin to examine their Christian stewardship concepts and understandings in a broader context and will begin to include planned gifts as well as current gifts in their stewardship response.
3. Members will be educated about the many gift opportunities for mission and ministry through their church.
4. Current contributions given in support of the ongoing annual budget will be freed up to strengthen and even expand existing programs.
5. The church and its various ministries and institutions will begin to receive major planned gifts that have previously been directed to other causes where planned-giving programs are already in place.

When your church encourages giving from one's accumulation (or assets), it is a way for the church to say:

- We believe in the future of this church.
- We want to be guided in our stewardship by our belief that all we have is a trust from God.
- We want to build a sense of permanence in what we do.
- We want to be good stewards as a church family, even as we expect each member to be a good steward.

What Is Planned Giving?

The concept of planned giving is not new, although the term may be new to many people. Such giving, referred to for years as deferred giving, has been primarily bequests given from wills and estates. The downside of deferred giving is that it limits a person's giving response by making the charity wait until sometime in the future to receive the gift. Planned giving, on the other hand, also includes giving from trusts, annuities, and the like. Planned giving makes it possible for a giver to make a decision now and give to the church immediately as well as later at some unspecified time in the future (after his or her death).

Planned Giving

- Giving outside the regular offering
- Giving for purposes beyond the general budget
- Giving from accumulation (or assets)

In many churches, planned giving is referred to as permanent fund ministry or endowment funds given to a church or other charity. Only the income from these funds can be spent. Gifts to endowment funds have occurred almost as far back as biblical times. However, this type of giving and accumulation by churches (and charities) has caused some consternation and arguments regarding the accumulation of funds when the church needs money now to pay bills. Some people are concerned that giving to endowments limits a person to giving later (after his or her death), when that person might be encouraged to make an estate gift now.

Where does it say that when I give my tithe (10 percent) and keep the rest (90 percent), I have accomplished my stewardship? Stewardship is not about 10 percent, but 100 percent of who and what I am in response to God's grace in Jesus Christ. That means that my stewardship is fulfilled not only in giving through the offering, but also includes what I accumulate.

Planned giving includes all of the above. It is the gifting from one's accumulation or assets, usually outside the regular offering, for purposes often beyond the day-to-day needs of the church.

Characteristics of a Planned Gift
- Given from accumulated assets
- Larger in size than annual gifts
- Complements other forms of giving

Objections abound in congregations regarding planned giving and especially endowments. The myth exists in finance circles that any form of designated giving (giving outside the budget) or endowment giving takes from the regular giving to the church budget. In the book *Money Matters: Personal Giving in American Churches* (Westminster John Knox Press, 1996; page 72), a research book on giving in local churches, the authors say they cannot find any correlation either way that such giving increases or decreases the amount a person will give to the regular offering of the church. My own studies have shown that when people make an extra gift, such as a planned gift, their giving to the regular budget of the church increases. Giving from one's assets or accumulation actually complements other forms of giving.

The members of East Emmanuel Church were proud of the little cemetery adjacent to the church grounds in the small town. They paid $2,000 a year to care for the grounds around the cemetery, which stretched their already-tight budget. The church moved in three years from paying for the maintenance and upkeep of the cemetery from the annual budget to funding it through planned gifts to the endowment fund.

I have heard stories about and have seen churches where the accumulation of investments in an endowment fund or a large gift from an individual to the church has had dire consequences to other giving in the church. In each case I have studied, the problem was not in the amount of the gift or of the endowment, but in the vision of the members for ministry and in the policies (or lack thereof) for the use of those funds.

What Can Be Given?

When we say that planned gifts come from accumulated assets, what is meant by that? Many people have significant amounts of cash in their homes, in bank accounts, in certificates of deposit, or in other forms of money market accounts. One of the most significant investment vehicles for people who are retired today are certificates of deposit. These retired people have experienced the Great Depression, so they have little trust in equity investments. The investments they have may provide only a modest return, but they know the money is there if they need it. People can give from these cash accumulations, but this may not be the wisest source of gifting. A better idea is to list the church as a co-owner. The owner of record can receive the income, control the investment, or cash it in at any time. Then when the person dies, the amount left in the investment goes to the co-owner, the church. This method of giving is often a secure way for a person to make a gift to the church and still retain a strong sense of security.

Gifting of cash may not always be the best gift to make. If a person has an asset that has appreciated in value, such as stock or real estate, such investments, if given to charity, could avoid all taxation. Rick's stock gift (mentioned earlier) was worth $1,000 more as stock than if it had been cashed in.

What Can Be Given?

- Cash
  - Certificates of deposit
  - Bank accounts
  - Liquid assets
- Appreciated assets
  - Stocks or bonds
  - Real estate
  - Personal property
- Life insurance
  - Existing policies
  - Cash value in policies
  - New policies
- Gifts of life income
  - Gift annuities
  - Living trusts
  - Charitable remainder trusts
- Retirement or pension assets

To help faithful stewards expand their vision of what they might give, Wayne Barrett, in his book *The Church Finance Idea Book* (Discipleship Resources, 1989; page 94), sets out a plan to help potential givers understand the ABC's of giving. I have tried this with church leaders, and it works. Have a group go through the list of potential gifts for each letter of the alphabet that a person can make. After I went through this list with a group of church leaders, a man approached me following the meeting. He said he had a boat that had been sitting in his back yard for three years without being used. He had thought his children would return home and enjoy spending time on the lake. "You mean I could give the boat to the church?" he asked. After some further investigation, he gave the boat to the church, and the church realized a gift of $3,500 on something that had been gathering dust (and weeds).

Planned gifts can be given during one's lifetime or after one's death. The gift may be a transfer of an asset to the church while a person is still living, or it may come from the proceeds of the cash value of a life insurance policy after a person has died. The gift may be given through a trust or through a life-income arrangement. Gifts may be completed at death through a dollar or percentage gift in a will, or through the transfer of a right (that is, property) from an arrangement made prior to one's death.

How Do You Begin a Planned-Giving Ministry?

When talking to church leaders about the benefits of a planned-giving ministry for their church, I have been surprised by the number of times I have been asked why anyone should consider giving more to the church. Some hesitate in giving a major gift to the church because they have not been convinced that the church has managed well what has already been given. As the church, we must realize that we have a stewardship, too.

For people to consider giving a major gift, they must be sure that their gift will be received appropriately (according to their desire when making the gift), and that it will make a difference. It is somewhat easy to make a gift through the offering for the operation (or survival) of the church, but giving a major gift takes an intentional act of faith and trust on the part of the giver. If a person does not feel that the church is managing its stewardship appropriately, major gifts or planned gifts will be slow in coming. Being intentional about telling the community of faith about how good a steward church leaders are will go a long way in building trust in givers.

Faithful stewards who are giving from their accumulation, either now or in the future, need a vision of how those funds will be used. What is your church's vision for people to give planned gifts? To have a goal of so many dollars in an endowment fund sometime in the future is not a vision that inspires giving. People want to know what will happen because of their planned gift. They need images and models to which they can give. One church, whose budget adjustments always included dropping maintenance items, raised a vision of a maintenance fund through the endowment. People who designed, built, and supported the construction of a building are often more interested in preserving the building than are others. Give them a vision of a maintenance fund that will perpetually maintain the building they had the vision to build. A gift of $25,000 invested at 4 percent will provide $1,000 of income every year for the maintenance of the church.

Institutions, colleges, hospitals, and homes have a goal to provide a maintenance endowment in the same amount of the cost of construction. I have never figured out why churches do not. When you build a building, endow the maintenance of that facility when you build it. Begin now to create an endowment to fund the maintenance of the building. Raise funds equivalent to the insured value of the building. These funds can never be dropped from the church's budget in order to balance the budget.

Invite people to give to scholarship funds through the church. Many churches have visions of providing support, especially to those people in their church who go into some form of Christian vocation. Others who see missions as the primary reason for the church's existence might give to a missions endowment. Others might give through their estate a value that would endow their annual gift to the church. For example, if I am giving $25 a week to the church now, a gift through my estate of $32,500 will eternally provide for my weekly giving to the ministry of the church.

Create a climate for making planned gifts through your church. People who give from their accumulation want to make sure their gift will make a difference. If church leaders always present a picture of a church in crisis, or if they threaten that the church doors will be closed if funds are not given, their messages will deter giving, not only now but most especially for the future. If you are unsure the church will be around after your death, why would you want to make a major gift to an endowment for the church?

Believe in Planned Giving

To have an effective planned-giving ministry, you must believe that planned gifts are possible. If you doubt that people have the assets to give—and even if they have the assets, you doubt they would make such gifts—your church will not receive any planned gifts. It does not mean your members will not make planned gifts. They will. But they will make them elsewhere.

The church has operated for years on the myth that all our people are without worth. (That is different from worthless.) Basically, we are still operating on the belief that our members have just enough to squeeze by. In their wonderful book *The Millionaire Next Door: The Surprising*

Secrets of America's Wealthy (Longstreet Press, 1996), Thomas Stanley and William Danko clarify who the millionaire in American society really is. We often think millionaires live in big houses, drive expensive cars, and go on extended vacations. Stanley and Danko portray millionaires as the people next door who live in meager houses, drive three-year-old cars, and rarely take expensive vacations—the perfect portrait of many church members.

Believe in the potential of your congregation and you will be amazed at the possibilities. Americans are increasing their assets at a phenomenal rate at the same time their earned incomes are at limits for giving. According to a popular radio broadcast, 1986 was the first year in which there were 1 million millionaires in America. In 1995, there were approximately 5 million millionaires.

The net worth of your members is increasing. Do you remember the figures mentioned in Chapter Four? The definition of rich in America has increased from $17,000 annual income in 1950 to $135,000 annual income in 2000. Would one in every ten households in your congregation qualify? one in every twenty? one in every thirty? What could be your congregation's potential?

In the book *Myths of Rich and Poor*, Michael Cox and Richard Alm show how the typical family's wealth is increasing. The net worth of households, not including home equity or other real property (adjusted for inflation), has been increasing each decade across the American culture:

Household Net Worth
Adjusted for Inflation

1970	$ 33,007
1980	$ 64,847
1990	$118,488
1997	$211,923

(*Myths of Rich and Poor: Why We're Better Off Than We Think*, by W. Michael Cox and Richard Alm; page 13. © 1999 by W. Michael Cox and Richard Alm. Reprinted by permission of Basic Books, a member of Perseus Books, L.L.C.)

As assets increase, as net worth grows, and as we age, more and more individuals are seeking the assistance of financial professionals (CPAs, financial planners, attorneys) to design the best way to preserve their assets as long as they live and to provide for immediate and appropriate transfer of assets when they no longer need them (at death). What place will your church be in when your members make estate planning decisions?

If you have been convinced that your church could benefit from planned gifts, make your own planned gift. Your effectiveness in asking someone else to do something you have not done yourself will be limited. Make your own discovery of a unique gift you could make. Or, at the least, redo your will and make your church a beneficiary of a percentage gift.

Promoting Planned Giving

As you know from surveying your church leaders, the reason people do not make planned gifts is because they have not thought about it. If the leaders have not included the church in their plans, how can they expect anyone else to include the church as a beneficiary of their will or estate plans? Churches have organized the finest committees, constructed the best policy statements, selected the wisest investment counselors, and have still failed to get any planned gifts for their ministry.

Why Many Programs Fail

1. Unclear vision
2. Not knowing who will give
3. Not planning far enough into the future
4. No budget
5. Lack of patience
6. Focus on annual, not on long-term
7. Lack of passion
8. Lack of promotion

Ruth was a missionary, a pastor's wife, and a dedicated member of her church. When she died she left a significant estate, most of which went to charity. Nothing went to her church. Why not? Why had she not included her church in her estate plan? People do not leave estate gifts to their church because they do not know they can leave such gifts.

Having an endowment program is a major first step. Recruiting a committee and setting up the policy to organize the endowment program in your church is the second and most important step, for all of this is of no use if no one gives you anything to fund the program.

Paint a vision for giving through your church's planned-giving program. Why should anyone make a gift to your church's endowment program? Start with your church leaders. If someone left your church $10,000 or $250,000 next week, what would your church do with the money? What dreams or vision do church leaders have for the money someone might give?

Show people what would happen if they left an estate gift to your church. Establish a policy for the distribution of gifts through your church, and let possible donors know what would happen if they gave to the church. People want to know that their gifts will make a difference and not just be absorbed into the regular church expenses.

Give people a vision to grab their attention. One such vision might be to help people convert their current giving into a lasting support of the church: "Your support of the church could be immortal. If you are giving a weekly gift of $35 to the church and you left a gift of $45,500 through your will, that gift (when invested at 4 percent) would continue to make your gift to the church each year forever." Or give a vision regarding the maintenance of the church: "One possibility of your giving through your will might be to the church's maintenance fund. For those of us who built the church, it is only right that we maintain the church we decided to build. A gift of $50,000 to the endowed maintenance fund of the church will provide at least $2,000 annually for the maintenance and upkeep of this great building."

Provide on a regular basis articles in the church newsletter about giving to and through your church's program of planned giving or endowments. Tell what could happen if you had these funds. Better yet, tell stories of what is already possible with these funds. If you have a scholarship fund, highlight stories about the recipients when they get the scholarship. Tell how much difference it will make in their lives. Have recipients send the church letters you can print in the newsletter twice a year about what is happening because your church's gift allowed them to attend school. After people have graduated, invite them periodically to send letters to the church about what is happening in their lives because your church allowed them to attend school.

If your church has other programs or services that benefit from the planned-giving ministries, find ways to tell stories of what is happening because of the gifts. People give because giving makes a difference, not just because the church says to give.

Make it year-round. If you tell people only once about your program, you have wasted your time. Any announcement Sunday morning will reach only a fraction of your congregation because the audience is different each week. Each publication will be received by members differently, according to where they are in their physical, emotional, and spiritual lives. You never know when you are saying the right thing at the right time. To be effective, any program of promotion must be year-round. Have you ever seen an advertisement in a newspaper or on television only once? No. Advertisements are repeated many times. Tell about your program when people are ready to respond. Repetition is essential.

Two to four times a year have people who have either made a gift or have included the church in their will or estate plan tell the congregation in the Sunday worship service why they have decided to make that gift of faith. When a person tells his or her reasons, it makes the possibility of others giving more of a reality.

At some point consider an endowment newsletter, which may be done quarterly, but no less than twice a year. Report stories of what is happening because of people giving through your program. Get people to tell why they have included the church in their plans. Provide articles on ways of giving (for example, giving through insurance or real estate or securities). Provide a place for people to respond in the newsletter:

> ❏ I want more information about _____.
>   (*Each time suggest a brochure or booklet you can provide.*)
> ❏ I have included the church in my estate plan.
> ❏ I would like to talk to someone about making a gift.

Provide a place for those who are interested to give you a name, address, phone number, and so forth. Be sure to include an address where they can send the response.

Once a year have an Endowment Sunday observance. Select a time when attendance is usually high. Do not combine this observance with a memorial observance, but select a time to focus just on the endowment program. If you give out scholarships, plan to present the recipients of the scholarships their awards on Endowment Sunday. Invite other people to tell their stories. Consecrate gifts that have been received since the last observance. List the results of the grants that have come out of those gifts over the past year. Invite people to celebrate this ministry with their commitment to include the church in their will, to make a special gift, or to talk to a professional about making an estate gift.

Promotion is not a sometime activity. You will probably not know when someone is going to meet with an attorney or financial planner to update an estate plan. Tell your story continuously. You may not know when someone is thinking he or she has some extra income or when an asset is about to be turned into cash. Promote planned giving possibilities all the time. If you do not tell your story, if you do not keep the possibilities of giving from one's assets in people's consciousness at all times, you may never receive a planned gift.

Focus on who will respond. Who is most likely to respond to your church's planned-giving program? Although we want all people to know about the program of planned giving and the options for responding to their faith, all people will not respond. Direct some information to the entire congregation; however, if you want a response, focus on those who will respond.

Look first at those who are givers. Those who are supporting your church with their gifts are more likely to include the church in estate plans than those who are not supporting the church. Those who have made significant gifts over time are more likely to include the church in estate plans than those who have made minor gifts. Those who are active in the church are more likely to give than those who are on the fringe of the church's life.

The older we get, the more we think about our mortality. People who are older (55 plus) and those who have been around the church are more likely to respond than those who are younger and newer members of the church. Single people, especially widows and widowers, are more likely to think about a gift to the church in their estate plans than those who feel an obligation to a surviving spouse or family.

Write articles about why people should give through the church's endowment program. Answer questions that people might ask: What if I give an undesignated gift? What if my selection for a gift is no longer needed (such as a gift for the bus fund and then the church eliminates the busing program)? Tell what will not happen with any gifts to these funds:

will not be used to pay electric bills, salaries, or whatever is appropriate to your church's vision. However, remember that people will respond better to what will happen with their money than to what will not happen.

Brochures are a way of life today. A wide variety of brochures is available for local churches. (Contact The Planned Giving Resource Center, P.O. Box 340003, Nashville, TN 37203-0003 for a sample packet of planned-giving brochures.) Sending a letter and brochure to every member may not be the best use of your resources. Be selective about the people to whom you send the brochures. Send them to those who are most likely to respond, or to those who have asked for a brochure on a specific subject.

Marketing, Motivating, and Giving

Promotion is focusing on the beneficiary of your services. It is a process of knowing those beneficiaries, caring about them, identifying their perceived needs, and finding ways to intersect your services with their needs.

Promotion and marketing are two sides of the same coin. Sometimes we tend not to like the term *marketing* in the church. However, we must learn to recognize the purpose of marketing and promotion as primarily a ministry as we help people make faithful decisions about their stewardship of accumulation. Then it is clear that marketing and promotion are indeed the intentional work of your planned-giving committee. Increasing the financial resources available for your church's ministry becomes an important, but secondary, purpose.

There is a difference between marketing and selling. Selling identifies what you need and tries to convince people to give it to you in exchange for something you can offer them. Marketing, or in this case planned-gifts promotion, is helping people complete their stewardship by making faithful decisions about the accumulation that God has allowed them to keep. It is understanding the people who are most likely to make gifts, caring about them, and building relationships with them, even if it means helping them to make planned gifts outside the church.

Have you ever been to Wal-Mart? When you enter a Wal-Mart store, the first person you meet is a greeter. That person's primary responsibility is to make you feel good and comfortable about being in Wal-Mart. Your church's planned-giving ministry needs a greeter to be effective. That person loves people and keeps them happy about your church by making phone calls, sending little notes, and visiting members. The greeter may know little about which planned gifts are possible, but he or she can let your committee know that someone wants to make a planned gift.

Everyone in your church can make a planned gift; however, not everyone is likely to do so. Some of your promotional work needs to be sent to everyone. A one-line reminder in the bulletin or newsletter can be directed to everyone. After all, you never know when someone might be changing a will or planning to sign a living trust that might include your church. Make a decision that all bulletins, newsletters, and other regular publications of your church will include at least a one-line sentence about giving from accumulation. Review the list of possibilities on page 80; then let your leaders brainstorm other ideas for the list.

For the general public, including people who are not in church every week, find ways to promote planned gifts on a regular basis. At least once a quarter, place in your church newsletter articles on some way to make a planned gift. The five-year plan at the end of this chapter (pages 92–94) gives an example of a time schedule in which to mail brochures. But do not mail only brochures. Always include an introductory letter about the subject of inviting people to consider the possibility of giving through ways suggested in the brochure (wills, trusts, real estate, and so forth). Be specific in the mailing.

> Thank you for your attendance at the estate planning seminar last week. Because of your interest, we want to provide you with more information about _____. If we can help you in any way in your faith giving, please contact _____.

Arrange to have a supply of planned-giving brochures on hand at the church any time someone wants information on a specific subject. Arrange to have a planned-giving bulletin board in a place where people going into or out of church are most likely to see it. Make it colorful and use large print. Do not overload the board with too much information. Cut and past articles from your newsletter. Put the one-liners about giving in large print. Set up a place to display one or two of your brochures. Make sure you change the selection of brochures often.

Schedule planned-giving seminars for possible donors. People are often hesitant to speak to legal and financial-planning advisers on their own because they are afraid of the potential cost or of appearing ignorant on a given subject. A seminar will give them a chance to hear a presentation, ask questions, and still remain anonymous to the adviser. For many people this may be the first opportunity they have had to speak to a financial specialist.

In one church, three times more men than usual attended the men's group meeting when an attorney came to talk to about "Men and Estate Planning." Some men stayed an extra thirty minutes after the presentation to ask the attorney questions. People are hungry for information.

Plan seminars related to people's interests. A seminar about estate planning for men, women, or seniors will get people's attention more than a generic seminar about estate planning. Send a general announcement to everyone. Then send invitations to specific people you think would respond to the seminar. Those who attend seminars are saying they have an interest, so follow up seminars with other publications: a newsletter, a letter with additional information, a brochure, and so forth.

Develop your plan. If you wait for someone else to tell the story about giving through the planned-giving program of your church, no one will give. Develop a written plan, with a detailed timeline for each step in your plan. Without a plan, you will not get anything done. With a plan, there is hope. Remember that the first word in any plan of promotion is *patience,* for it takes time. Just because you are ready to tell people about the exciting possibilities of planned giving does not mean they are ready to respond. Plan your work and work your plan.

Books and articles on estate planning point to the statistic that 50 to 70 percent of the people who die each year do not have a valid will (*The Planned Giving Idea Book,* by Robert F. Sharpe; Thomas Nelson Inc., 1978; page 100). Without a will, they cannot make a gift to your church. A serious educational program for all ages on the need for wills is a must for your church's promotion of planned giving.

Include one-line stories of giving in every bulletin, newsletter, or any publication that goes out from the church. You may even include one of them at the bottom of the church's letterhead. Some one-liners might include:

- Have you included the church in your will?
- Does your living trust include the church?
- Jane's will gives 10 percent of her estate to the church. What have you done?
- Did you know you could make the church a beneficiary of your life insurance policy?
- Did you know that you could include the church as a beneficiary of your I.R.A.?
- Does your pension plan allow for the inclusion of the church as a beneficiary after all other beneficiaries have been cared for?
- Do you have a life insurance policy that has cash values that you no longer need? Did you know you could give them to the church?

One church that used to receive estate gifts asked me why only one estate gift had been given to the church during the past five years. (The gift was from a non-member.) In exploring their situation, it was discovered that twenty-five years ago there was a policy that all bulletins, letterhead, and newsletters would include the simple phrase "Have you included the church in your will?" Somehow over the years that phrase had gotten lost in their publications, so people forgot to include the church.

The sample five-year plan on pages 92–94 is designed to be used at the beginning of a church's planned-giving program, but it can be adapted by any church. If your church is just beginning, start with Year One. If your church has had a program going for some time, begin with Year Two or Three. After you have completed the five-year plan, start again with the plan at Year Two. Or better yet, use this model to design a plan that is more specific to your church and community of faith.

Five-Year Planned-Giving Promotional Plan

Whenever someone makes a gift, get permission from the giver or the family to tell the congregation about the wonderful response of faith. (Ordering information for resources listed in this plan is on page 109.)

Year One

- Make a presentation to church leaders twice a year about possibilities and responses. Invite the leaders to make a planned gift.
- Put one-liners about giving in all church bulletins and newsletters.
- Place an article in the church newsletter on planned giving each quarter.
- Plan two seminars (October and March) on wills and estate planning.

Year Two

- Make a presentation to church leaders twice a year about possibilities and responses. Invite the leaders to make a planned gift.
- Plan and celebrate a Memorial Sunday observance.
- Put one-liners about giving in all church bulletins and newsletters.
- Place an article in the church newsletter on planned giving each quarter.
- Send two planned-giving mailings:
    1. The importance of estate planning and the benefits of making a gift through the church (send to entire congregation). Send a brochure on recording your estate wishes, such as *Suggestions Upon My Death: A Final Gift of Love,* to those who respond.
    2. The opportunity of giving through estate planning (send to entire congregation). Send the brochure *Why Should I Include the Church in My Will?* to those who respond.
- Plan three seminars:
    February: general seminar on wills and estate planning
    May: estate planning for women
    October: estate planning for men

Year Three

- Make a presentation to church leaders twice a year about possibilities and responses. Invite the leaders to make a planned gift.
- Put one-liners about giving in all church bulletins and newsletters.
- Place an article in the church newsletter on planned giving each quarter.
- Plan and celebrate a Memorial Sunday observance.
- Plan an Endowment Sunday celebration.
- Design two endowment newsletters to be sent to everyone:

1. Theme: Let Me Introduce You to the Endowment Program of This Church
   2. Theme: You Can Be a Philanthropist (Tell stories of what others are doing. Help people see how they can give.)
- Send three planned-giving mailings:
   1. The opportunity of giving through estate planning (send to entire congregation). Send the brochure *No Will–No Way* to those who respond.
   2. Brochure *Ways to Give at Year End* (send to entire congregation in December)
   3. Brochure *Giving Is an Act of Faith* (send to leaders, committee members, and the top 25 percent of givers)
- Plan four seminars:
   January: Can I Afford to Retire? (including time on estate planning)
   March: general seminar on wills and estate planning
   May: financial planning (including wills) for parents
   October: general seminar on wills and estate planning

Year Four
- Make a presentation to church leaders twice a year about possibilities and responses. Invite the leaders to make a planned gift.
- Put one-liners about giving in all church bulletins and newsletters.
- Place an article in the church newsletter on planned giving each quarter.
- Plan and celebrate a Memorial Sunday observance.
- Plan an Endowment Sunday celebration.
- Design three endowment newsletters to be sent to everyone:
   1. Theme: Let Me Introduce You to the Endowment Program of This Church
   2. Theme: You Can Be a Philanthropist (Tell stories of what others are doing. Help people see how they can give.)
   3. Theme: Ways I Can Give Through My Estate
- Send three planned-giving mailings:
   1. The opportunity of giving through estate planning (send to entire congregation). Send the brochure *No Will–No Way* to those who respond.
   2. Brochure *Ways to Give at Year End* (send to entire congregation in December)
   3. Brochure *Basic Estate Planning Tools* (send to leaders, committee members, and the top 25 percent of givers)
   - Plan two seminars (October and March) on wills and estate planning.

Year Five

- Make a presentation to church leaders twice a year about possibilities and responses. Invite the leaders to make a planned gift.
- Put one-liners about giving in all church bulletins and newsletters.
- Place an article in the church newsletter on planned giving each quarter.
- Plan and celebrate a Memorial Sunday observance.
- Plan an Endowment Sunday celebration.
- Design three endowment newsletters to be sent to everyone:
  1. Theme: Let Me Introduce You to the Endowment Program of This Church
  2. Theme: You Can Be a Philanthropist (Tell stories of what others are doing. Help people see how they can give.)
  3. Theme: Can a Living Trust Help Me Assure My Financial Security and Make a Gift to My Church?
- Send three planned-giving mailings:
  1. The opportunity of giving through estate planning (send to entire congregation). Send the brochure *Giving Through My Will* to those who respond.
  2. Brochure *Ways to Give at Year End* (send to entire congregation in December)
  3. Brochure *Giving Is an Act of Faith* (send to leaders, committee members, and the top 25 percent of givers)
- Plan two seminars (October and March) on wills and estate planning.

Chapter Eight

Memorial and Honor Giving

The purpose of the gift-planning strategy of a local congregation is to facilitate a person's desire to give. Some people want to give and have only the income from their gifts used for specific projects. We discussed such gifts, known as endowments (sometimes as permanent funds), in Chapter Seven. Now we are ready to consider another part of the planned-giving strategy, the memorial gifts or honor gifts that the givers intend to be used immediately for specific projects.

Memorial and Honor Funds

Most churches have some form of memorial fund. Memorial gifts traditionally are given instead of flowers when a person dies. The invitation to give ("in lieu of flowers") is often listed in the obituary. The memorial gift is a way to say that the person was important and will be missed. Memorial gifts do not always have to come when a person dies. Some people make memorial gifts on the anniversary of someone's death, or in remembrance of someone close to them. Gifts that become part of the memorial fund do not have to be in remembrance of someone who has died. Sometimes gifts are given to honor someone who is still alive. This gift, called an honor gift, is a celebration of one's life at an anniversary or birthday, or just to say thanks. One person I know has a close aunt who is more than eighty years old, yet is vibrant in all she does. She does not need any more gifts. In fact, she is in the process of giving away many of her items of worth. On the anniversary of her birth, a gift is given in honor of her through the memorial funds for youth ministry (her favorite).

The most common problem with these memorial and honor funds is that most of them are not used, which discourages people from giving. In fact, many churches have memorial funds between $5,000 and $25,000 that were given years ago and no one can remember what they are for.

Does your church encourage gifts through your church's memorial funds? The scenario in most churches is that when Mom died, the children decided that since Mom sang in the choir for many years and the choir needed new robes, that would be a lasting tribute to Mom. The obituary in the paper instructed people to make memorial gifts to the church in lieu of flowers. A total of $2,500 was given for the new robes that cost $3,500. Then the memorial committee waited for the rest to come in. That was seven years ago, and they are still waiting. Meanwhile, the family has left the church in anger over the memorial never being completed.

The problem in most churches is that there is not a committee or policy for memorial gifts. One person manages the funds, which are usually in a bank savings account. No one is really in charge. The family in the scenario above probably never received a report of the progress of the fund. In other cases, money has been given but no communication has been made with the family to decide how it is to be spent. In still other cases, churches simply put the funds in the general account of the church, so the money is lost. People know that there is a fund and that money has been given, but since they never see any of the money being spent for any program, mission, or ministry of the church, they do not see any need to give more money.

So what can the church do? Institute a six-month memorial policy. With such a policy, all funds must be spent within six months of a person's death or within six months of the money being given to the church in memory or honor of someone. The church must communicate with a representative of the deceased or honored person within six months to talk about what is to become of the money that has been given. If there has been no declaration of intent, the church can make suggestions regarding the use of the money. If the family selected a use for the money and not enough was given to purchase the selected item, the family should be given a choice: 1) select a new item for the memorial that is consistent with the amount that has been given; or 2) add the additional funds to fulfill their gift selection. In most cases, the family will raise the rest of the funds. They have chosen a proper memorial, and they will find a way to make it happen.

Remember, however, that the leaders of the church should control gift selection. Most people do not know what the church needs. In an article titled "The Care and Feeding of Memorial Funds," Frederick Leasure states that people think the church needs what they can see. That is usually something to do with worship: a brass cross, a brass candlestick or candelabra, or brass communion ware. However, the church can use only so much brass.

The leaders of the church should decide annually what kinds of gifts they would like to receive in the coming year through the memorial and honor gift fund. Include in the list items that cost a lot. Maybe the church needs a new computer system ($30,000). Also include small gifts. You may want to put Bibles in each of the classrooms ($15 each). Include program gifts (vacation Bible school or youth ministries) as well as potential mission gifts (Habitat for Humanity, your church's mission in Africa). List the gifts as well as the cost of each gift. If you have a current (or near-future) building program, include such gifts to the new building as chairs, podiums, sound systems, and so forth that may be given in memory of or in honor of a loved one. Revise the list annually, if not more often.

Six Elements of a Memorial Fund

1. Appropriate and immediate responses to donors and family
2. A public and permanent record of the name of the person being remembered
3. Adherence to policy on the use of such funds
4. Complete annual reports to the congregation
5. Both immediate and annual recognition of the person being remembered
6. Annual contact with the deceased person's family

The Memorial and Honor Committee

Organization is key to any program or ministry in the church. Recruit at least three people to be part of the memorial and honor committee. When you have just one person, not much gets done besides keeping the accounts. When you have two people, they sit and talk about all they cannot get done. With three people, there is enough discussion to get things moving.

Give each member of the committee something to do. If you have three people, one person can be in charge of marketing. Marketing is the work of helping people in the congregation know that they can make gifts through this fund and how the gifts are used. The second person can be in charge of sending thank-you notes to those who give and a recognition of a gift received to the family of the person who is being remembered or honored. The third person can keep good records of who gave, how much, and how the money has been spent.

Set up a system to let people know that a gift has been received. Work with a printer to design a memorial card for your church. Within a week of a gift being made, send a note of appreciation to the person who made the gift. This note goes a long way toward inviting people to make other gifts. On the other hand, when people do not know whether their gift has been received, they may not give again.

All gifts should be recorded in a memorial record book. This book is often an album that is set out for all to see. Send a report of the gifts received to the family of the deceased or to the person being honored. You do not need to tell the value of each gift, just who gave it. A periodic report of the progress of the funds received will encourage the family to make additional gifts, if they are needed. Make sure the family knows that something has been done with the money that has been given.

The accounting person on the committee should keep close records throughout the year. Keep a record of members and friends of the church who have died during the past year. Also keep a record of people who have died who are related to members and friends of your church. You may also want to include people from your community or the world who have died. Select a time each year to recognize those people who have died during the year and to consecrate the gifts put into the ministry of the church through the memorial and honor fund. There are several times in the year when a church may celebrate Memorial Sunday. Some celebrate on All Saints' Sunday, which is the first Sunday in November, but any Sunday will work.

A Memorial Service of Recognition

Invite all whose lives have been touched by those you will memorialize to come to the Memorial Sunday service of recognition. In addition to putting notices in your church bulletin or newsletter, send personal invitations to those who represent people who have died. On the day of the service, consecrate the gifts that have been placed into service in the ministry of your church during this past year as a result of memorial gifts. Find a way to praise God and thank people for a life lived and for the ministry of your church.

Celebrate the Saints in Worship

- Focus worship on thanksgiving to God for the lives of local people and well-known figures, such as Susanna Wesley or Francis of Assisi. God was glorious in them, and we long for a continuing sense of communion with them as we proclaim in the Apostles' Creed.
- Choose music your congregation can do meaningfully. Use "For All the Saints" if it is familiar. If not, try "Faith of Our Fathers" or "Forward Through the Ages." (Then plan to use "For All the Saints" in worship at another time so that your congregation can learn it.)
- Tell stories about the people in your congregation who have died. Include in the sermon brief remembrances of local saints who lived in other times. A useful source is *For All the Saints: A Calendar of Commemorations for United Methodists* (edited by Clifton F. Guthrie; Order of Saint Luke Publications, 1995).
- Have a banner-making session during Sunday school a week or two before the memorial celebration. Invite the youth and children to help make banners of saints' names. Also include members of your congregation who have died in the past several years. Display the banners in the sanctuary.

- Read the names of those who have died. Ring the church bell after each name is read. Plan for the congregation to respond after each name with words such as these: "We thank you, God, for this person's life among us."
- Celebrate Holy Communion, which reminds us that the living and the dead are always together in Christ. Use the Great Thanksgiving prayer for all saints (*The United Methodist Book of Worship*, pages 74–75).

A Memorial Brochure

People want to give, but they often need ideas to spark their action. They will not give, and often cannot give, unless they are given a means to give. Design a special memorial brochure to have available at the memorial service. You will want to include in the brochure ways to give and types of gifts needed, as well as how to give and where. In the first panel of the brochure, list the ways people can give through your memorial fund.

- **Memorial Gifts**—The most common way to give is to make a gift to the church at the time of the person's death. Some of us may have wanted to make a gift at the time of death, but never got around to it. If we did not make a gift then, is there a way for us to make a gift later? Many people also would make a gift on the anniversary of the person's death, or at the time they would have celebrated his or her birthday each year. If you do not give people permission to give gifts, they will not do so.
- **Honor Gifts**—Most people would not think of making a memorial gift when a person is still alive. Give them permission to make a gift through your church's fund while the person is still living. Give them suggestions: a person's birthday, anniversary, or just a time when they are thinking of that person. Why wait until someone is dead to say how important he or she is?

Your church will want to control the types of gifts you receive. In the second panel of your brochure, make a list of the gifts the church needs and the estimated costs of the gifts. Include not only large gifts but also individual gifts almost anyone can afford. Make sure to update the list annually and to report to the congregation when gifts are received.

The third panel of your brochure should include a place to record the giver's name, address, phone number, and so forth. Also include a place to record who is to be remembered or honored, the amount of the gift, and the gift chosen. Allow the giver to choose from the list of church needs, to choose from gifts chosen by the family, or to name a gift of his or her own choice.

The most important part of this brochure is often left out. You may assume that everyone knows where the church is located, but do not assume that. Put the church's address and phone number on the brochure where everyone will see it. If people do not have an address to mail the gift to, you will not receive it.

Give a brochure to everyone who attends the memorial service. Find other ways during the year to give the brochure to everyone in the church, and ask them to keep it until they need it. Put extra copies of the brochure in a location in the church where people will walk by and may pick one up. You never know when someone is thinking about making a gift.

Do not forget the funeral home. Every funeral home has a storage area full of brochures for making gifts to funds and societies. Why isn't your church part of that supply of memorial possibilities? The funeral director is the first one the family will talk to about making a memorial gift, for it is usually a question funeral directors ask as the obituary is being written for the newspaper. Funeral homes usually have a place where visitors can sign in. Why not have your church's brochures on the podium where they sign in, so that members of your church and others may think to include your church in their memorial plans?

Conclusion

There Is a Long Way to Go

"**W**ow, that's exciting," Dave commented with a sigh at the conclusion of an especially invigorating Growing Giving Seminar. "But it was a bit overwhelming, too. Where do we start?"

It can be overwhelming when you read a book like this one or attend a seminar filled with so many new ways to think. One thing to remember is that you now have information, and you have thought about this topic more than anyone else in your church. The other church leaders, and especially the members of your church, may not be ready to make these changes, even if it will make a difference in the giving levels of your church.

Slowly bring people on board with new ideas. Remember Joiner's Law in Chapter One: "When the leaders lead, the congregation will follow." Select three people from your congregation, perhaps members of your finance committee, to read this book. Give one person a copy of the book and a list of the people you want to read the book. Ask that person to read the book within the next two weeks and then to pass the book on to the next person on the list. When the three people have finished the book, meet with them to discuss what you learned and how it applies to your church. With that small group you can prepare the following three steps to changing the way your church finances ministry.

1. Analyze Your Current Situation

The place to begin is where you are. What are the assumptions that now guide your funding-ministry system? This conversation may take some time because so many of our assumptions are ingrained into the way our church has operated for a long time. Identify your assumptions by asking, "Why do we do things the way we do them? What is the true result of the way we do things?" It may be hard, but now is the time to be completely honest with yourselves. Look objectively and honestly at your congregation's ways of operating.

As you are looking at the way you do financial stewardship, make a list of what is working well. Discuss why the things you are doing work well. Caution: Do not go too far back in your church's history to find the things that work well. What went well even ten years ago may not apply to your situation today.

Look at your publications, letters, and articles about finances in your church. If you were an outsider or a new person in your church, what message would you get from these writings? Be objective.

Compare your church's yearly finances over the past five years. Then make the comparisons on a monthly basis. Look at both the income (and its sources) and the expenses. Is there a trend? Have there been some identifiable times when income increased? What happened during those times to motivate people to give more? Is there something from the past that gives a clue about how your church will respond in giving in the future?

Do a demographic study of your church. What is the age of your congregation and the makeup of your church? Compare people's giving history over the past five years. Is there a pattern? Are the same people giving well? Is there an identifiable group who consistently is not giving, or not giving well? Why? How is your church unique? If you were to divide your congregation into four or five groups of people, what groups would you identify? Would you put them into groups because of their giving or because of their activity or involvement? What can you learn from those groupings?

2. Build a Plan

With this picture of your current reality, where do you want to go? What changes do you want to make in the way your church funds ministry?

If you know where you are (current reality) and you make a list of where you want to go, the next step is to make a plan for how to get there. Chapter Two ("Developing a Strategy for Funding Ministry," pages 21–26) will be helpful here. You may want to go back and review that chapter to remind you of what you may want to do.

As you plan, consider some of the key points from this book:

- Instead of focusing on raising money, focus on helping people be Christian stewards (Christian philanthropists).
- Beginning where you are, develop a three- to five-year plan for your annual finance program.
- Discuss ways to involve people during the year in knowing where their money is going. Help them see that their giving is appreciated and makes a difference.
- Invite people to give in ways that make them feel good, make a difference, and provide a lasting impression on their faith. Decide how many times a year you will give people an extra way to give.
- Design a strategy to inform people about giving beyond the budget, beyond earned income, and beyond their comfort zone. If you help people give beyond what they normally can and do, they will grow in their faith. People who give from their assets (give a major gift) are giving for faith reasons, and they are fulfilled.

3. Develop Stewards (Philanthropists)

If your goal is to raise money to pay bills, you are doomed to failure. If you focus on the bills and the money that is needed, you will continue to move in ways that will be against the grain of faith—and of your people. However, if your goal is to help develop stewards (Christian philanthropists), your work will move in a different manner. Developing stewards centers on the individual and each one's faith journey, even in giving. The needs of the church to receive funds is a secondary goal.

What do you need to do to center on the needs of the individual, rather than on what he or she can do for the church? This book is about making Christian philanthropists. It outlines five key ingredients of that ministry:

1. It recognizes that individuals are unique.
2. It understands the interests and needs of individuals.
3. It develops and interprets ministries consistent with each person's needs and interests.
4. It seeks to develop an ongoing relationship with individuals.
5. It converts interest into action.

How can you assist people in your church to become Christian philanthropists?

The financial ministry of the church is more than money. It is a way of growing faithful stewards and helping God's plan for this world to come about. And it is fun. Good luck!

Bibliography

Theology of Stewardship

God the Economist: The Doctrine of God and Political Economy, by Douglas M. Meeks (Minneapolis: Fortress Press, 1989).

Stepping Stones of the Steward: A Faith Journey Through Jesus' Parables, by Ronald E. Vallet (Grand Rapids: William B. Eerdmans Publishing Company, second edition 1994).

Stewards Shaped by Grace: The Church's Gift to a Troubled World, by Rhodes Thompson (St. Louis: CBP Press, 1990).

Financial Stewardship

Afire With God: Spirit-ed Stewardship for a New Century, by Betsy Schwarzentraub (Nashville: Discipleship Resources, 2000).

Christians and Money: A Guide to Personal Finance, by Donald W. Joiner (Nashville: Discipleship Resources, 1991).

Don't Shoot the Horse ('Til You Know How to Drive the Tractor): Moving From Annual Fund Raising to a Life of Giving, by Herb Mather (Nashville: Discipleship Resources, 1994).

Generous People: How to Encourage Vital Stewardship, by Eugene Grimm (Nashville: Abingdon Press, 1992).

Get Well! Stay Well! Prescriptions for a Financially Healthy Congregation, by Wayne C. Barrett (Nashville: Discipleship Resources, 1997).

How to Increase Giving in Your Church, by George Barna (Ventura, CA: Regal Books, 1997).

Money Matters: Personal Giving in American Churches, edited by Dean R. Hoge (Louisville: Westminster John Knox Press, 1996).

More Money, New Money, Big Money: Creative Strategies for Funding Today's Church, by Wayne C. Barrett (Nashville: Discipleship Resources, 1993).

The Abingdon Guide to Funding Ministry: An Innovative Sourcebook for Church Leaders (Volumes 1, 2, and 3), edited by Donald W. Joiner and Norma Wimberly (Nashville: Abingdon Press; 1995, 1996, 1997).

The Church Finance Idea Book, by Wayne C. Barrett (Nashville: Discipleship Resources, 1989).

Miscellaneous Stewardship Resources

Behind the Stained Glass Windows: Money Dynamics in the Church, by John and Sylvia Ronsvalle (Grand Rapids: Baker Books, 1996).

Choices and Challenges: Stewardship Strategies for Youth, by Dan R. Dick (Nashville: Discipleship Resources, 1994).

Clergy Personal Finance, by Wayne C. Barrett (Nashville: Abingdon Press, 1990).

For All the Saints: A Calendar of Commemorations for United Methodists, edited by Clifton F. Guthrie (Akron: Order of Saint Luke Publications, 1995).

Gift of a Lifetime: Planned Giving in Congregational Life, by J. Gregory Pope (Nashville: Broadman & Holman Publishers, 2000).

Gifts Discovery Workshop, by Herb Mather (Planned Giving Resource Center, 615-340-7076).

Holy Smoke! Whatever Happened to Tithing? by J. Clif Christopher and Herb Mather (Nashville: Discipleship Resources, 1999).

Myths of Rich & Poor: Why We're Better Off Than We Think, by W. Michael Cox and Richard Alm (New York: Basic Books, 1999).

Putting God First: The Tithe, by Norma Wimberly (Nashville: Discipleship Resources, 1988).

Revolutionizing Christian Stewardship for the 21st Century: Lessons From Copernicus, by Dan R. Dick (Nashville: Discipleship Resources, 1997).

The Crisis in the Churches: Spiritual Malaise, Fiscal Woe, by Robert Wuthnow (New York: Oxford University Press, 1997).

The Millionaire Next Door: The Surprising Secrets of America's Wealthy, by Thomas J. Stanley and William D. Danko (Atlanta: Longstreet Press, 1996).

Finance Campaigns

Called to Serve (LeWay Resources, 800-725-3929).

Celebration Sunday (LeWay Resources, 800-725-3929).

Consecration Sunday (Cokesbury, 800-672-1789).

In the Light of God's Grace (Resource Services, Inc., 800-527-6824).

Pony Express (Stewardship Resources, Inc., 800-234-5844).

"Seeking Something Better," in *The Abingdon Guide to Funding Ministry: An Innovative Sourcebook for Church Leaders* (Volume 2), edited by Donald W. Joiner and Norma Wimberly (Cokesbury, 800-672-1789).

Special Delivery (LeWay Resources, 800-725-3929).

"Stewardship Fair," in *The Abingdon Guide to Funding Ministry: An Innovative Sourcebook for Church Leaders* (Volume 1), edited by Donald W. Joiner and Norma Wimberly (Cokesbury, 800-672-1789).

The Joy of Belonging (Resource Services, Inc., 800-527-6824).

The Joy of Discovery (Resource Services, Inc., 800-527-6824).

The Quill (Church Fund Raising Services, 800-826-2048).

Planned-Giving Resources

(The following resources are available from The Planned Giving Resource Center, The General Board of Discipleship, P.O. Box 340003, Nashville, TN 37203-0003. Phone: 615-340-7076.)

Achieving Dreams Beyond the Budget: How to Increase Giving in Your Church

Stewardship: A Rainbow of Possibility

Planned Giving Sample Packet (Includes the following brochures. The brochures may also be ordered separately.)

- *Basic Estate Planning Tools*
- *Giving Is an Act of Faith*
- *Giving Through My Will*
- *No Will–No Way*
- *Suggestions Upon My Death: A Final Gift of Love*
- *Ways to Give at Year End*
- *Why Should I Include the Church in My Will?*

Books by Discipleship Resources may be ordered on the Internet bookstore (http://www.discipleshipresources.org) or by calling 800-685-4370.

For more information about stewardship, visit the General Board of Discipleship Web site (http://www.gbod.org/stewardship).